# Fifty Shades of Green

# Fifty Shades of Green

## COOKING WITH CANNABIS

**Deborah Champlin**

ISBN-13: 9781981262342
ISBN-10: 1981262342

# Disclaimer

The contents of this book are for informational and historical purposes only and are not intended to treat, diagnose, or prescribe. The book is not intended to be used as a replacement for diagnosis or treatment by a competent medical professional.

It is assumed that you live in a state where cannabis or medical cannabis is considered a legal substance.

All herbs in combinations or individually have been used traditionally and historically and are described to you for educational purposes only.

*I dedicate this book to all people who were told to go home and get their affairs in order because there was nothing else they could do.*

# Contents

Acknowledgments · · · · · · · · · · · · · · · · · · · · · · · · · · · · · · · · · · · · · · · · · · · · · · · · · · · · · · · · · xiii

Introduction · · · · · · · · · · · · · · · · · · · · · · · · · · · · · · · · · · · · · · · · · · · · · · · · · · · · · · · · · · · · · xv

A Brief History of Cannabis · · · · · · · · · · · · · · · · · · · · · · · · · · · · · · · · · · · · · · · · · · · · · · · 1

How Cannabis Affects the Body · · · · · · · · · · · · · · · · · · · · · · · · · · · · · · · · · · · · · · · · · · · 5

Gaining Access to Quality Cannabis · · · · · · · · · · · · · · · · · · · · · · · · · · · · · · · · · · · · · · · 7

How to Create Therapeutic Dosages · · · · · · · · · · · · · · · · · · · · · · · · · · · · · · · · · · · · · · 11

Methods of Ingesting · · · · · · · · · · · · · · · · · · · · · · · · · · · · · · · · · · · · · · · · · · · · · · · · · · 15

Tools and Equipment · · · · · · · · · · · · · · · · · · · · · · · · · · · · · · · · · · · · · · · · · · · · · · · · · · 17

Weights and Measurements · · · · · · · · · · · · · · · · · · · · · · · · · · · · · · · · · · · · · · · · · · · · 21

Extracts and Concentrates · · · · · · · · · · · · · · · · · · · · · · · · · · · · · · · · · · · · · · · · · · · · · 25

Using Other Medicinal Herbs and Essential Oils · · · · · · · · · · · · · · · · · · · · · · · · · · · 42

Recipes · · · · · · · · · · · · · · · · · · · · · · · · · · · · · · · · · · · · · · · · · · · · · · · · · · · · · · · · · · · · · · 44

Edibles, Savory ···································································· 47
   Compound Cannabis Butters ································· 49
   Cannabis Pesto Sauce ········································· 51
   Cannabis Hot Sauce ············································ 52
   Cannabis Chimichurri Sauce ································ 53
   Cannabis Mayonnaise ········································· 55
   Cannabis Hollandaise Sauce ································ 57
   Cannabis Vinaigrette Dressing ····························· 59
   Cannabis–Raspberry Vinaigrette ·························· 60
   Cannabis Aioli ···················································· 61
   Cannabis Croutons ············································· 63
   Cannabis Wiener Schnitzel ·································· 64
   Cannabis Spätzle ··············································· 67
   Baked Pineapple and Cannabis ·························· 68
   Rosemary and Garlic Focaccia (Roman Flatbread with Cannabis) ·· 69
   Sausage and Cannabis Soufflé ···························· 70
   Sweet and Spicy Spacy Nuts ······························ 73
   Spiced Cannabis Pecans ····································· 74
   Dizzy Chex Mix ·················································· 75
   Dizzy Onion Chex Mix ········································ 76
   Dizzy and Sweet Chex Mix ·································· 77
   Cannabis Herbed Rice ········································ 79

Edibles, Sweet ····································································· 81
   Dizzy Fudge ······················································ 83
   Dizzy Caramels ·················································· 84
   Sweet 'n' Salty No-Bake Cannabis Peanut Butter Bars ·· 85
   Salted Caramel Sauce ········································· 87
   Cannabis Chocolate Drops ·································· 89
   Pot Brownies ····················································· 91
   Double Chocolate Chip and Cannabis Cookies ······ 93
   Double Chocolate and Cannabis Cupcakes ··········· 95
   Chocolate Cannabis Buttercream Frosting ············· 96

Cannabis Gingersnaps · · · · · · · · · · · · · · · · · · · · · · · · · · · · · · · · · · · · · · · · · · · · · · · · · · 97
Cannabis Lemon Bars · · · · · · · · · · · · · · · · · · · · · · · · · · · · · · · · · · · · · · · · · · · · · · · · · · 99
Apple Raspberry Cannabis Bars · · · · · · · · · · · · · · · · · · · · · · · · · · · · · · · · · · · · · · 100
Cranberry Orange Cannabis Cake Bites · · · · · · · · · · · · · · · · · · · · · · · · · · · · · · 102
Cannabis Sunshine Muffins · · · · · · · · · · · · · · · · · · · · · · · · · · · · · · · · · · · · · · · · · · · 103
Cannabis Pecan Pie · · · · · · · · · · · · · · · · · · · · · · · · · · · · · · · · · · · · · · · · · · · · · · · · · · · · 105
Basic Cannabis Pie Dough · · · · · · · · · · · · · · · · · · · · · · · · · · · · · · · · · · · · · · · · · · · · 106
Canna Banana Bread · · · · · · · · · · · · · · · · · · · · · · · · · · · · · · · · · · · · · · · · · · · · · · · · · · 107
Dizzy Monkey Bread · · · · · · · · · · · · · · · · · · · · · · · · · · · · · · · · · · · · · · · · · · · · · · · · · · 108
Cannabis Pine Bark · · · · · · · · · · · · · · · · · · · · · · · · · · · · · · · · · · · · · · · · · · · · · · · · · · · · 109
Cannabis Chocolate-Dipped Strawberries · · · · · · · · · · · · · · · · · · · · · · · · · · · · 111
Cannabis Marshmallow Treats · · · · · · · · · · · · · · · · · · · · · · · · · · · · · · · · · · · · · · · · 113
Oatmeal Raisin and Cannabis Cookies · · · · · · · · · · · · · · · · · · · · · · · · · · · · · · · 114
Canna Butter Cookies · · · · · · · · · · · · · · · · · · · · · · · · · · · · · · · · · · · · · · · · · · · · · · · · · 115
Cannabis Pound Cake · · · · · · · · · · · · · · · · · · · · · · · · · · · · · · · · · · · · · · · · · · · · · · · · · 117
Cannabis French Toast Strata · · · · · · · · · · · · · · · · · · · · · · · · · · · · · · · · · · · · · · · · 118
Cannabis Jell-O · · · · · · · · · · · · · · · · · · · · · · · · · · · · · · · · · · · · · · · · · · · · · · · · · · · · · · · · 121
Cannabis–Vanilla Bean Ice Cream · · · · · · · · · · · · · · · · · · · · · · · · · · · · · · · · · · · 122
Port-a-Pot Ganache · · · · · · · · · · · · · · · · · · · · · · · · · · · · · · · · · · · · · · · · · · · · · · · · · · · 124
Ganja Ganache · · · · · · · · · · · · · · · · · · · · · · · · · · · · · · · · · · · · · · · · · · · · · · · · · · · · · · · · 125
Cannabis Marshmallows · · · · · · · · · · · · · · · · · · · · · · · · · · · · · · · · · · · · · · · · · · · · · · 126
Cannabis Chantilly Cream · · · · · · · · · · · · · · · · · · · · · · · · · · · · · · · · · · · · · · · · · · · · 127
Cannabis Lollipops · · · · · · · · · · · · · · · · · · · · · · · · · · · · · · · · · · · · · · · · · · · · · · · · · · · · 129
Dinner and a Movie · · · · · · · · · · · · · · · · · · · · · · · · · · · · · · · · · · · · · · · · · · · · · · · · · · · 131

Menu · · · · · · · · · · · · · · · · · · · · · · · · · · · · · · · · · · · · · · · · · · · · · · · · · · · · · · · · · · · · · · · · · · · · · · 133

Resources · · · · · · · · · · · · · · · · · · · · · · · · · · · · · · · · · · · · · · · · · · · · · · · · · · · · · · · · · · · · · · · · · 135

Common Equivalents · · · · · · · · · · · · · · · · · · · · · · · · · · · · · · · · · · · · · · · · · · · · · · · · · · · · 137

Appendix · · · · · · · · · · · · · · · · · · · · · · · · · · · · · · · · · · · · · · · · · · · · · · · · · · · · · · · · · · · · · · · · · 139

# Acknowledgments

would like to thank my husband for his unconditional love, support, and encouragement and for just "knowing" that I could do this even when I had doubts. Without him, this book would not have been possible. I would like to thank my friend Patty, for her curiosity and infectious energy that inspired me to write this book, and Marvin, for his excitement and confidence in what I am doing. I would also like to thank my family and friends for their love and support (especially my mom, who's my biggest advocate). I would like to thank God for placing this amazing healing herb on this earth for us to use for our minds, bodies, and souls and for saving my life!

Roxana Gonzalez/Shutterstock.com

# Introduction

As an herbalist and from my own experience, I consider cannabis to be the most powerful healing herb on the planet. I have seen this plant help so many people, which is why I am driven to dispel the myths and downright lies about cannabis. With the new regulations coming down the pike, it will be difficult and costly for a person with cancer to obtain an effective dosage to battle his or her condition. That's one of my reasons for writing this book. If you learn the basics, you will be able to create exactly the dose you need.

As far as the future, I want to see an end to cannabis prohibition, sensible legalization, and minimal regulations. Last but not least, I'd like to see complete reparations for those unjustly incarcerated for violating nonsensical cannabis laws based on purposely inaccurate cannabis science.

I used cannabis for the first time many decades ago but never truly understood how effective this medicinal herb could be or how great an effect it would have on the rest of my life.

In my earlier years and somewhat today, the dark cloud of cannabis prohibition was always present: the insane laws, the black market, the hours upon hours of wasted time and energy—never mind the money and costs—associated with all of that. I spent decades knowing I was breaking the law and doing something wrong by society's standards and conflicted in my head that I wasn't. How could this be wrong? I was less stressed, happier, more joyful, more excited about life, and a don't-sweat-the-small-stuff kind of girl. I am still all of that to this day.

I have a healthy relationship with this herb. It saved my life and many other lives and will continue to do that as long as it is on earth.

The reason I am so passionate about all herbs is because they're intelligent. They are a smart, healthy choice, and I know firsthand that they work. Cannabis, like other medicinal herbs, is less toxic to your body and mind than synthetic pharmaceuticals, never mind a more affordable option.

Here is the magnitude of the effect cannabis has had on the rest of my life. I really shouldn't be sitting here right now writing this book. I'm sure I would have been dead by now if it weren't for cannabis. In 1999 I was diagnosed with a condition called Barrett's esophagus. I had been living with periods of unexplained pain for decades. When I initially went to the doctor, this condition was happening more often and more painfully than ever before. I was in chronic pain that would come on suddenly and last for hours. Instead of being uncomfortable and annoying pain, it was now excruciating, mind-numbing, scary pain!

I made an appointment with a gastroenterologist, who performed a procedure called an endoscopy. This is a procedure where the doctor uses specialized instruments to view internal organs. In my case, the doctor looked at my stomach and esophagus. It's an awful procedure to go through and requires you to be sedated but awake. Oxymoron?

The first thing I remember the doctor saying to me after the procedure was, "Thank God you came in when you did." He said that I had a good chance that the pain was cancer of the esophagus. What a statement! Luckily, when the biopsy results came back, I had dodged a bullet. I was diagnosed with Barrett's esophagus, one stage below cancer. The doctor said that I would need to come back in three months for another endoscopy. In case you are wondering what Barrett's esophagus might be, here is the definition from the Mayo Clinic:

In Barrett's esophagus, tissue in the tube connecting your mouth and stomach (esophagus) is replaced by tissue similar to the intestinal lining. Barrett's esophagus is most often diagnosed in people who have long-term gastroesophageal reflux disease (GERD)—a chronic regurgitation of the acid from the stomach into the lower esophagus. Only a small percentage of people with GERD will develop Barrett's esophagus.

Barrett's esophagus is associated with an increased risk of developing esophageal cancer. Although the risk is small, it's important to have regular checkups for precancerous cells. If precancerous cells are discovered, they can be treated to prevent esophageal cancer.[1]

The doctor prescribed the purple pill called Nexium and told me that I would have to take it the rest of my life! It was so expensive (at the time, seven dollars a pill) and loaded with side effects. My insurance wouldn't cover the cost because it was a new drug, and there wasn't a generic version. When I couldn't afford the prescription any longer, I had to resort to using an over-the-counter drug called Prilosec OTC.

So it was a happy accident that I found how well cannabis worked when one night I had an episode. I was out of Prilosec, and it was late in the evening. I knew that if I didn't do something, I would be in pain the entire night and would probably wake up with the same pain. I remembered that I had made some cannabis-infused fudge, and it was in the freezer. My thought was to eat a piece to see if I could just sleep through the pain. So I ate a piece of cannabis fudge and got ready for bed. Within thirty minutes or so, I noticed that the pain wasn't escalating (like it normally did), and I thought I should take another piece. After another thirty minutes, the pain was completely gone. I couldn't believe that the pain was gone.

The next day I was reeling with the newfound pain reliever, and my thoughts were racing on other ways to use cannabis, since smoking never gave me relief from the Barrett's flare-ups. I looked at all the forms of ingestion, like tinctures, edibles, glycerites,

---

1 Mayo Clinic - https://www.mayoclinic.org/diseases-conditions/barretts-esophagus/symptoms-causes/syc-20352841

lotions, and lip balms, to name a few. I prefer the tincture of cannabis, which is a liquid cannabis extract. It is convenient, low calorie, and discreet, and most importantly, it works like a charm. I noticed it was hard to find quality and consistent dosage, so I decided to make my own.

Once I perfected my formula, I shared it with my husband, who suffers from pain from two separate back injuries resulting in two separate back surgeries. He had been smoking cannabis for pain, but when he tried the tincture and later the creams I made, he was amazed at how well they worked at controlling his pain. It has now been seven years, and when you ask about my episodes, I say, "What episodes?" When you ask my husband what his pain level is, he says (at the exact time of this writing), "A two." I guess you can ask yourself, "Whom do I know who has had two back surgeries and can say that his or her pain level is two?"

This has been an amazing journey, and we are so happy that we are not consumed with pain and sickness. I am a believer that cannabis has saved us, and I believe it can and will help so many people suffering in so many ways. I love that it is a natural substance and is an alternative to expensive and toxic pharmaceuticals. My hope is that you will consider using cannabis for your health and wellness and that this book will guide you to the facts enabling you to make and customize remedies for yourself and your family.

I recently watched the first-ever Cannabis Health Summit. It was a two-day conference with over twenty speakers. There is so much information about cannabis and its real health benefits. How do I keep from overloading someone who is reading this for the first time? My reason for writing this cookbook hasn't changed after the Cannabis Health Summit, and the reason for this cookbook is to empower others to understand the what, why, and how of using cannabis as a healthy nutritional and medicinal supplement. I like the old adage "teach a man to fish." Once you understand how beneficial this herb is for your body, mind, and spirit, I hope you will look to this book for guidance in creating your own confections, and I hope to possibly inspire you to learn as much as you can about how this amazing plant is necessary for your health.

Using cannabis in food is not really that difficult, although dosage can be a little tricky. But once you have the basic items prepared, it is quite easy to incorporate them into any dish you can imagine and control the dosage, too. Aunt Sandy of *Aunt Sandy's Medical Marijuana Cookbook* said that she cooked an entire Thanksgiving dinner all with cannabis. I can't imagine what the guests looked like after eating all that food!

Since completing a family herbalist and culinary arts program, attending Oaksterdam University, and creating wonderful things that helped friends and family with pain and other issues, I felt compelled to share how to DIY! Besides, it's lovely to tailor ingredients to an individual or condition. It's also very rewarding to know that you have helped someone you care about. I am inspired every day to learn as much as I can about cannabis and all the different ways it can be used internally and externally. You may not know that you don't have to smoke it to get the nutritional and medicinal properties of the herb. As you read further, you'll see that consuming cannabis sublingually and topically gives you the biggest bang for your buck! And it is actually the most effective way to use this herb, in my opinion.

Lallemand, *Hemp Harvesting on the Rhine Bank. L'llustration, Journal Universel, Paris*, 1860. Marzolino/Shutterstock.com

# A Brief History of Cannabis

There is much to learn when it comes to the history of cannabis, and I urge you to look deeper into this subject on your own. It would be impossible to include it all here, so I have included some of my favorite links in the resources section of this book. Simply put, cannabis has been used as medicine and food for tens of thousands of years. Hemp was a dominant plant superior to cotton during the Industrial Age, but politics, money, greed, and an amazingly effective propaganda campaign drove this amazing plant into the abyss, where it has stayed for over seventy-five years.

Cannabis was used in some of the oldest forms of medicine making, including China, India, and America, to name a few, long before the pharmaceutical industrial complex was formed. In fact, cannabis was in the *US Pharmacopeia* from 1854 until 1941 and was a commonly used ingredient in many patented medicines.

It is believed that the first president of the United States, George Washington, planted, cultivated, and smoked cannabis and knew the value of this plant when it came to paper, canvas, oil, and many other industrial uses. Queen Victoria was prescribed a tincture of cannabis by her physician, Sir Joshua Reynolds, for her premenstrual syndrome. Even today, it is still effective for this condition.

## What Is the Difference between Cannabis and Hemp?

The simple answer is that cannabis is hemp, and hemp is cannabis. The genus or botanical name, *Cannabis sativa* (Cannabinaceae), is the same seed as cannabis hemp. In fact, the cannabis plant is related to the hops (Cannabinaceae) plant. There are different strains (Sativa, Indica, and the wild strain called Ruderalis), and they are all from the same family, *Cannabis sativa* (Cannabinaceae).

Two men burning marijuana in a field in Garner, North Carolina, in 1942. Everett Historical/Shutterstock.com

So I guess the next question would be, why did they outlaw this historic plant?

Great question! I'm so glad I asked.

There are many facets to the *why*, so here's a start.

Domestically and internationally, powerful organizations—such as Lammott Dupont, Standard Oil, Randolph Hearst, Weyerhauser, John D. Rockefeller, Eli and Harry Payne Whitney, and the US government (the who's who of the rich and famous)—had a lot invested in the synthetic petrochemical and pharmaceutical industry. By making these patented materials, they could sell them to multinational corporations that they owned for highly inflated prices and could dominate the market. Cannabis hemp was and still is its biggest threat.

## Why Would Cannabis Hemp Be Such a Threat?

Another great question!

Cannabis was and is inexpensive, easy, fast to grow, and renewable. For thousands of years, virtually all known paper came from hemp. No one ever cut down a tree to make paper. Today hemp paper is produced at one-quarter of the cost, is ten times stronger, and lasts ten times longer than paper from trees. It has been used as a textile for centuries and is far superior to cotton, but without technology, it is difficult to harvest and process.

In 1794 the invention of the cotton gin by Eli Whitney made cotton cheap to produce, on par with cannabis hemp. Then, in the 1890s, a new method of harvesting cannabis hemp called the Decorticator promised to put cotton back in its place as an inferior product. Cannabis hemp is twenty-six times stronger and lasts ten times longer than cotton and needs *no* chemicals to produce. (By the way, you need *half* of all the chemicals produced in American agriculture to grow cotton. Starting to see the picture here?) Well, in 1938, a *Popular Mechanics* article identified cannabis as the "New Billion-Dollar Crop."

The powers that be couldn't have that, since they were highly invested in nonrenewable commodities, like oil and chemicals. (Can you say Big Pharm?) So it was back to the dark ages for this amazing plant.

With more scientific research becoming available and anecdotal stories being shared, cannabis now threatens the cancer-medical complex and its billions in yearly profits. It is a cheaper and natural medicine that works. If cannabis can cure cancer, how would that affect the for-profit cancer industry? It really does look like it's more about wealth than health.

Canna Obscura/Shutterstock.com

# How Cannabis Affects the Body

First and foremost, there has not been a single death associated with cannabis overdose. If you understand what the plant is and how it works in the body, you will discover that it is very hard to use the amount needed to cause harm to your body and cause death. In fact, you would need to consume fifteen hundred pounds of cannabis in fifteen minutes to cause death. Really? That's almost a ton of cannabis. Who could possibly eat a ton of anything in fifteen minutes? Certainly using concentrated forms of cannabis can cause discomfort, but it isn't capable of stopping your heart, unlike some pharmaceuticals and narcotics.

Cannabis is an herb, not a narcotic or a so-called drug. Unlike pharmaceuticals, cannabis does not have the ability to override our central nervous system, and therefore it cannot override the core functions of the body, like breathing and a beating heart. When used thoughtfully, cannabis is complementary to our bodies and works with endogenous cannabinoid receptors that are found in every vertebrate's endocannabinoid system, including sea squirts and tiny nematodes.

So the cannabinoids found in the cannabis plant (brought to you by God) have antioxidant and anti-inflammatory properties, among others, which should tell us that it was put on Earth for us to use and can not only cure disease but also prevent disease and promote our health and wellness, body, mind, and spirit.

If you would like more information regarding the endocannabinoid system, please go to the Appendix section in the back of the book.

I feel it is important to also mention the craze of CBD-rich products. Researchers have found that isolating the CBD molecule and removing the molecules that people don't like, say THC, causes the CBD to be less effective. The scientist who discovered this phenomenon termed it the "entourage effect," meaning that each component of the plant needs the others to perform.

During the conference, I heard a speaker explain it like this, which is so appropriate for this cookbook: "We're making a cake, and we're using flour, sugar, butter, and eggs. Each one by itself doesn't really taste that pleasing. But put them together in the correct amounts, and you end up with a beautiful cake that tastes great!"

And that is how the whole cannabis plant works. Synergistic. In concert. All together.

Commercial grow of flowering cannabis plants close to harvest, California, 2017. SEASTOCK/Shutterstock.com

# Gaining Access to Quality Cannabis

This next step can be a bit challenging, and due to the popularity of extracts, it can be hard to obtain the amount of material needed to create concentrates for use in the following recipes.

If you don't have the pleasure of knowing a reputable organic grower or the opportunity to grow your own medicine, then another option would be to visit your local collective or dispensary and check pricing on leaf, trim, kief, or shake. In my opinion, using flowers is a waste of money, but they can certainly be used if money is no object to you or if you grow medicine that is never intended to be smoked.

Leaf and trim tends to contain large amounts of the medicinal components needed to create effective medicine for most adults. It is said that leaf and trim often contain one-eighth or more of the THC found in the flowers. In my experience of trimming pounds of cannabis, I believe this to be true. These trimmings can be valuable ingredients to a cannabis chef or cook. Plus the use of trimmings minimizes wasting any part of this beautiful plant.

All types and strains of cannabis can be used in preparing items for ingestion. Dosage considerations are very important, because the potency of the different strains of cannabis can vary greatly, and dosage is not an exact science. The recipes found in this publication are a medicinal dosage and are intended not to get a person high but to offer a sense of relaxation and pain relief. It is possible to create items that are too strong and cause discomfort or that are too weak and have no effect. Proper dosage is a high priority—no pun intended—when creating any item that is to be eaten (as a solid) or taken sublingually (as a liquid). With a good understanding of how cannabis works, one can create healing and healthy concoctions that will be greatly appreciated by your body and by the ones you love.

## Types of Cannabis

**Fan/sun leaves:** These are the larger leaves from the plant, which are cut off during the vegetation and/or flowering stage.

**Sugar trim:** These are the smaller leaves usually covered with trichomes, which are removed from the flower after the plant has been cut for further processing.

**Flowers/buds:** These are the actual flowers produced by the female plant, which is harvested and dried before becoming ready to consume.

**Shake:** These are the leftover bits and pieces after the flower has been dried. Shake is usually very small pieces, similar to tea leaves.

**Kief:** These are the actual trichome glands removed from the plant during processing.

**Ice hash:** This is the result of a process of using water and ice to freeze the trichomes from the leaf matter. The cannabis trichomes are heavier than water, which allows for collecting a large number of glands from the leftover trimmings.

**Hash oil:** This is the result of a process of either applying pressure and heat or using a solvent to dissolve the trichome glands and then allowing the solvent to evaporate, leaving a pure rosin or oil.

**Rosin:** This is the result of a process of extracting the trichomes via carbon dioxide.

In a recently published science paper it found that the endocannabinoid
system is involved in essentially all human diseases.
— DR. RAPHAEL MECHOULAM

Shutterstockphoto3/Shutterstock.com

# How to Create Therapeutic Dosages

A therapeutic dose of cannabis is intended not to get the person high but to relieve pain and inflammation, which tends to lead to better sleep. I remember a doctor saying, "People don't die of old age but of old-age-related illnesses, number one being inflammation." Cannabis is one of the most powerful anti-inflammatory plants in the plant kingdom. I call it the queen of all medicinal herbs, and when it is combined with other safe medicinal herbs, you can create some truly amazing products that greatly reduce inflammation, among so many other things.

As I mentioned earlier, dosage consideration is important. The rule of thumb is to start low and go slow. It is possible to over-medicate on cannabis. I think the word "overdose" is too strong a word, since we understand cannabis can't stop your heart, but overmedicating can make you feel pretty awful. You might even feel like you're dying, but you're not. The effects of overmedicating shouldn't cause you to become alarmed, but they can include dizziness, nausea, vomiting, rapid heartbeat, extreme drowsiness, feeling like time stands still, and/or fainting. Food-based cannabis medicines can affect each person differently, which is especially true for inhaled methods. Long-term cannabis smokers can fall prey to overmedicating when using edible cannabis products. If this has happened or happens to you, the cook must take responsibility for making something so strong and not informing you how much to ingest. With responsible use and care, overmedicating should never happen.

If you have overmedicated, it is important to remain calm, not panic, stay hydrated, and eat something, if possible. Eating will help to absorb some of the cannabis that has been consumed. Your symptoms should improve within a few hours. I promise and just know that edible cannabis used with care is safe and will not cause any long-term toxicity.

The term "titration" refers to a method of gradually adjusting the dose and analyzing how you feel until you have reached the desired level of relief. So the correct way to titrate a medicinal dose of edible cannabis that you are unfamiliar with is to start with one-quarter of the portion (cookie, candy, brownie, etc.) and wait for an hour and analyze how you feel. If you feel no effect, consume another one-quarter of the portion and wait another hour. Repeat this process until you begin to feel a sense of relaxation. Once you know the potency of the edible, you can just eat that total amount the next time you need relief.

Ingesting cannabis takes longer to show its effects, and the effects vary from person to person. It is important to use the titration process, as it will prevent any side effects of overmedicating. Another plus of creating your own remedies is that you will be able to stay consistent with the dosages, and titration will not be necessary from batch to batch.

Dose considerations will vary based on the amount of THC in the cannabis, the size of the person, and the experience of the person using it. You do build up a slight tolerance over time, which is normal and may require you to use slightly more. As herbalists, we have been trained to not use herbal remedies on a daily basis unless dealing with an acute health issue. For treating chronic problems, it is recommended to use herbal remedies for six days in a row with the seventh day off. I personally use Sunday as my day off to let my body rest and catch up.

Of all the 300,000 species of plants on Earth, no other plant source can compare with the nutritional value of CANNABIS/HEMP/MARIJUANA seeds. It is the only plant on Earth that provides us with the #1 source, and the perfect balance of essential amino acids, essential fatty acids, globulin edestin protein, and essential oils all combined in one plant, and in a form which is most naturally digestible to our bodies.
— JACK HERER'S, THE EMPEROR WEARS NO CLOTHES, A $100,000 CHALLENGE!

Africa Studio/Shutterstock.com

# Methods of Ingesting

There are so many different ways to ingest cannabis. Food items and liquids can be used to extract the medicine from the plant material. This goes for all herbs.

The most common method of ingesting is smoking the dried flower of the female cannabis plant. Since this is a cookbook, I will not spend any time on this method. Besides, if you remember, my condition was not treated effectively by smoking cannabis. We will spend time learning about the following three methods of consuming cannabis: by skin, by stomach, and by mouth.

## Skin

Our skin is the largest organ of the body. It is capable of absorbing and excreting many toxins and waste. With that said, healing balms, lotions, and massage oils made with ingredients you can literally eat are wonderful and effective ways to use cannabis topically. They have helped relieve arthritis, inflamed muscles, and many types of skin conditions, and using a topical does not get you high.

## Stomach

It is scientifically proven that 80 percent of our immune system is found in our gut. So you feel how you eat. Most humans these days have immune systems that are not functioning properly. Hence, disease. This is where I had my epiphany. With a gastrointestinal disease, cannabis is amazing at soothing the upset, as I know firsthand. Eating food items infused with cannabis is another good way to consume cannabis. You can also pay attention to ingredients and the quality of those ingredients to customize foods to your tastes and likings.

## Mouth

This is now my preferred method. It is the most convenient and works fast. The best way I can describe it is that "It's liquid, not solid." In this method, the cannabis works with the glands of the mouth and assimilates faster than by eating food items, and you can get excellent control of the dosage. Tinctures, mists, vinegars, and tonics are this type of sublingual method of ingesting cannabis. Really, these are my favorites!

TierneyMJ/Shutterstock.com

# Tools and Equipment

These are the tools and equipment that I use regularly. I will offer alternatives to items that are costly or hard to find. Most every household with a cook in the kitchen will have these items. I will also share links to resources I use consistently. Another consideration is to be knowledgeable about food safety. Completing a ServSafe course is highly recommended and will give you a good understanding of handling food safely. You can visit the National Restaurant Association Educational Foundation, www.servsafe.com, for complete ServSafe certification guidelines.

Always use glass and/or stainless-steel cookware. It's up to you if you want to dedicate cookware to just cannabis cooking. I don't do this, because glass and stainless clean up like new. I don't have residue left on the cookware. It's a personal choice, though.

## Glass Blender

Do not use an overly high-speed blender because it blends too fast when incorporating ingredients. I use a standard blender with a glass pitcher free of chips and cracks. Glass is the preferred container because it is nonporous and easier to clean.

## Crock-Pot

I have a couple of small Crock-Pots. You can use a large one, but usually it is too much pan for the amount of mixture these recipes will produce. I found small ones at a local big-box store for around ten dollars each.

## Other Tools

Other tools you will need are the following:

- Coffee grinder
- Medium and small saucepans—stainless steel
- Measuring spoons—stainless steel
- Measuring cups—stainless steel
- Large and small saucepans—stainless steel
- Food scale
- Glass jars and lids (all sizes, depending on what you're making and how much. I use mason jars and keep an eye out for them to go on sale.)
- Wax or parchment paper
- Stainless-steel strainer, fine mesh
- Stainless-steel strainer, regular
- Unbleached coffee filters without the glued edge
- Cheesecloth
- Spatulas
- Spoons
- Silk screen, ultrafine, twenty-five microns
- Latex-free, no-powder surgical gloves
- Paper towels
- Tincture bottles for travel
- Jars or lotion bottles
- Permanent markers and white tape—for identification
- Whisks, small and large
- Flexible oven-safe silicone candy molds, various shapes and sizes

Pressed hempseeds create a highly nutritious oil, containing high amounts of essential fatty acids.

Barry Blackburn/Shutterstock.com

# Weights and Measurements

This is the most important part of cooking with cannabis. It is crucial to understand the ratio of cannabis in order to produce consistent extracts. Once you understand and are consistent, you will not find it necessary to titrate each time you make a new batch of something. I personally like to make certain items that will allow one to enjoy more than a bite of something, but mostly these items are created for therapeutic effect only and not to get high.

I use different types of cannabis depending on what I am making at the time. For alcohol-based ingredients, I like to use leaf or sugar trim. The leaves and sugar trim of the cannabis plant contain cannabinoids but at lower concentrations than the flowers or buds. For butters that I will use in baked items, I like to use kief. Kief comes from the leaves and flowers of the cannabis plant and is just the dried trichomes, which have not had any additional processing. I find this a better application for baked goods, because you don't get the dark green color and chlorophyll aftertaste. It's really a personal preference, and you can use whatever you want. They'll all produce the same thing, extracts.

I use basic measurements and kitchen math when creating the bases for my recipes. I like to make my bases using the extra-strength amount, and because of this, I can dilute and add other ingredients without reducing the amount of medicine to a level that is nonexistent. The goal is to create a mixture that can be dosed low so that you can take more as you work up to the appropriate dosage for the condition. When creating topical applications, I always use the extra-strength recipe without diluting for best results.

Here are my measurements for preparing infusions, extracts, and concentrates based on an estimated cannabinoid content. If you are using material that has been tested, use that percentage in the formula.

A carrier can be butter, oil, alcohol, vinegar, or glycerin. When possible, always use non-GMO, organic ingredients.

## Percentage of Cannabinoids per Batch:

To determine the milligrams of cannabinoids in the batch, follow the formula below.

- **Fan/sun leaves** at approximately 5–7 percent = 50–70 milligrams cannabinoids per gram
- **Sugar trim** at approximately 10–12 percent = 100–120 milligrams cannabinoids per gram
- **Flower/bud** at approximately 15–20 percent = 150–200 milligrams cannabinoids per gram
- **Kief** at approximately 50–60 percent = 500–600 milligrams cannabinoids per gram
- **Ice hash/oil** at approximately 70–80 percent = 700–800 milligrams cannabinoids per gram
- **Rosin** at approximately 80–90 percent = 800–900 milligrams cannabinoids per gram

In the example below, if you use 4 grams of flowers/buds at 20 percent cannabinoids, or 200 milligrams per gram (see bulleted list above), and 16 ounces of unsalted butter, you will have 800 milligrams of cannabinoids per batch of butter or 50 milligrams per ounce of butter.

200 x 4 = 800 milligrams per batch of butter
800 ÷ 16 = 50 milligrams per ounce of butter

## Percentage of Cannabinoids per Serving:

To determine the milligrams of cannabinoids per serving, follow the formula below.

In this example, if you use 8 ounces of the infused butter in a recipe that makes forty cookies, you will have 10 milligrams per cookie.

8 ounces x 50 milligrams = 400 milligrams

400 milligrams ÷ 40 cookies = 10 milligrams or 1 gram per cookie

Once you understand the basic recipes, you can adjust the amount of plant material to suit your taste and medicinal needs.

ElRoi/Shutterstock.com

# Extracts and Concentrates

There are several ways to extract the trichome from the leaf of the cannabis plant, which will then allow you to add this substance to various recipes. I have tried every which way and have found the following to be the best and to my liking when creating different mediums. Plus these methods seem to keep the odor from taking over your kitchen, and I make it a priority to use organic, non-GMO ingredients when possible.

Cannabis is fat and alcohol soluble, meaning it will infuse easily into substances like butter, milk, oils, and alcohol. Glycerin and vinegar need a little extra help to infuse the medicinal properties of the plant. The process of decarboxylation (conversion through heat) is key to activating the acid components of the plant. The cannabis plant material is heated low and slow for a short period of time, allowing the decarboxylation process to covert the THCA into THC.

Ideally it is best to use the kief or hash oil in confectionary creations for a more desirable-looking edible. The different methods of extraction have their benefits and challenges. Although easy to make, some may have a strong odor when cooking, while others may take several weeks to prepare. But in my opinion, they are worth the odor and the wait.

Creative Family/Shutterstock.com

# Cannabis Flour

This is the easiest of all applications to prepare. After decarboxylation, place the material in a coffee grinder and grind to a powder similar to the consistency of flour. This grinding won't be necessary if using kief.

## Equipment Needed

- Coffee grinder
- Canning jar with lid for storage

## Ingredients

- 1 lb. any flour (including nut flour, bread flour, etc.)
- 1 tbsp. decarboxylated plant material, finely ground (low strength) or desired amount

## Directions

Mix the tablespoon of decarboxylated plant material into the flour of your choice. Adjust the amount to suit your taste and medicinal needs. Use as you would in any recipe calling for flour.

Bruce Weber/Shutterstock.com

## Dairy—Butter

I prefer to use kief when making cannabis butter. It is easier to work with. It's a cleaner process, and it keeps recipes tasting and looking closer to the real deal. The end result will be an infused cannabis butter that can be used in any recipe calling for regular butter and that freezes beautifully for later use.

## Equipment Needed

- Small Crock-Pot
- Spoon
- Silk screen
- Stainless-steel strainer, fine mesh
- Flexible mold

## Ingredients

- 1 lb. organic unsalted butter
- 1 tbsp. decarboxylated plant material (low strength) or desired amount

## Directions

Melt butter in a small Crock-Pot on low heat. Once slightly melted, add desired amount of kief. Mix well. It is important to make sure this mixture does not boil. Switch between the low setting and the warm setting to ensure this does not happen. Stir often; you are trying to melt the gland that holds the cannabinoids. The fat in the butter will slowly melt the gland, and stirring helps this process along.

Cook this mixture for at least 12 to 24 hours. You can turn this mixture off overnight and continue the process the next day. Once done, strain this mixture with the silk screen into a glass measuring cup and pour into molds. Place in refrigerator to set. Once set, remove and store in plastic bags labeled with the date and the dose. Use in place of butter for recipes. Store in a freezer for up to a year.

Africa Studio/Shutterstock.com

# Dairy—Milk (Bhang)

All milk, except nonfat, contains enough fat to dissolve the glands of the trichomes. This allows you to produce an extraction to use in ice creams, mousse, or any recipe that calls for dairy. Bhang is the method of adding cannabis to milk and heating it for a period of time. It has been used in India for centuries and is said to be the second most popular way to use cannabis. Once made, you can use it on cereal and in coffee creamer, cheeses, yogurts, and so on.

## Equipment Needed

- Small Crock-Pot
- Spoon
- Strainer, regular
- Coffee filter
- Canning jar with lid

## Ingredients

- 32 oz. organic milk (2 percent or whole) or heavy cream
- 1 tbsp. decarboxylated plant material (low strength) or desired amount

## Directions

Bring milk to a boil, reduce to a slow simmer, add desired amount of kief, and let simmer for 30 minutes. Do not boil! Remove from heat and strain out plant material. Then give the milk a final strain through the coffee filter. Store in an airtight container in the refrigerator as you would normal milk. It should last one week. It can be frozen.

Africa Studio/Shutterstock.com

# Oils

Since trichomes are fat-soluble, all types of organic, non-GMO oils work beautifully for extraction to use in food, and they are the base for most lotions and creams, among other things. Extracting the cannabinoids from the plant is the same process as extracting in butter.

## Equipment Needed

- Small Crock-Pot
- Spoon
- Silk screen
- Strainer, regular
- Canning jar with lid

## Ingredients

- 16 oz. organic oil (olive, coconut, avocado, etc.)
- 1 tbsp. decarboxylated plant material (low strength) or desired amount

## Directions

Heat oil in a small Crock-Pot on low heat. Once slightly warm, add desired amount of plant material. Mix well. It is important to make sure this mixture does not boil. Switch between the low setting and the warm setting to ensure this does not happen. Stir often; you are trying to melt the gland that holds the cannabinoids. The fat in the oil will slowly melt the gland, and stirring helps this process along.

Cook this mixture for at least 12 to 24 hours. You can turn this mixture off overnight and continue the process the next day. Once it is done, strain this mixture with the silk screen into a glass measuring cup and pour into jars. Use as you would any oil.

monticello/Shutterstock.com

FIFTY SHADES OF GREEN

## Alcohol

Cannabis is alcohol soluble and a versatile solvent. Infuse pure vanilla extract for use in various confections, and it can be used to make tasty tinctures. Cannabis can be infused in most alcohol, including Irish creams, brandy, gin, tequila, and so on.

## Equipment Needed

- Small Crock-Pot
- Spoon
- Silk screen
- Strainer, regular
- Canning jar with lid

## Ingredients

- 16 oz. alcohol of choice
- 1 tbsp. decarboxylated plant material (low strength) or desired amount

## Directions

Cold process: This preserves most of the constituents of the plant that are sensitive to heat. Place the alcohol and plant material in a jar with a tight-fitting lid. Shake mixture daily for 4 to 8 weeks. Strain, reserving liquid.

Hot process: This is the fastest method. Place alcohol and plant material in a Crock-Pot and slowly heat the mixture for 12 to 24 hours, stirring off and on. Do not allow the mixture to boil. Once it is done, strain and reserve liquid. It can be used as a tincture or in cooking.

Gayvoronskaya_Yana/Shutterstock.com

# Vinegars

Vinegars are resurging in the health and wellness movement. Once infused, they can be used in any application requiring vinegar. Vinegars are great for cleansing the body and can be infused with other medicinal herbs for a nourishing tonic.

## Equipment Needed

- Small Crock-Pot
- Spoon
- Silk screen
- Strainer, regular
- Canning jar with lid

## Ingredients

- 16 oz. raw organic vinegar, with the mother (Braggs is a good one)
- 1 tbsp. decarboxylated plant material (low strength) or desired amount

## Directions

Place the vinegar and plant material in Crock-Pot. Slowly heat the mixture for 24 hours, stirring off and on. Do not allow the mixture to boil. Once it is done, strain and reserve the liquid.

Creative Family/Shutterstock.com

# Honey

Honey is another medium that works great with cannabis. Once infused, it can be used any way you would normally use honey.

## Equipment Needed

- Small Crock-Pot
- Spoon
- Silk screen
- Strainer, regular
- Canning jar with lid

## Ingredients

- 16 oz. organic, raw local honey
- 1 tbsp. decarboxylated plant material (low strength) or desired amount

## Directions

Add the honey to the Crock-Pot and set on low. Gently warm the honey, and then add the desired amount of plant material. Cook for 24 hours. Do not allow the mixture to boil. Switching from the low to the warm setting should prevent this from happening. Strain while still warm and place in jars. Honey does not need refrigeration but can be refrigerated. Use in teas, coffee, baking, and so on.

Anny Studio/Shutterstock.com

## Decarboxylation of Plant Material
### Equipment Needed

- Sheet pan lined with parchment paper or nonstick baking mat

### Ingredients

- Desired amount of cannabis buds, flowers, leaves, trim, or kief

### Directions

Preheat oven to 325°. It is important that this temperature is exact. Use your oven thermometer to verify accuracy. Spread cannabis bud, leaf, trim, or kief on a sheet pan no more than an inch thick. If using bud, break apart. Place into oven until the first sign of smoke or 5 minutes, whichever comes first. It is important to keep an eye on this to prevent overcooking the cannabis. Remove from the oven and let cool, and then transfer to a glass jar. This cannabis is ready for use as a flour, spice, infusion into oils, and so on.

# Using Other Medicinal Herbs and Essential Oils

One of the things I enjoy most about creating herbal remedies is the ability to customize. There are many herbs that work complementarily to other herbs, and some help others to be absorbed into our systems faster and more efficiently. I teach a class about using common herbs found in most household kitchens to create first-aid remedies and other helpful remedies. Some can actually save your life. Below are a few of my standards and favorites that you will find in the recipes to follow. I have included sources for obtaining these herbs that are good to have on hand when needed, or if you're fortunate to be able to grow an herb garden, these are ones to become familiar with:

- Aloe vera
- Basil
- Burdock
- Calendula
- Cayenne
- Chamomile
- Chickweed
- Cinnamon
- Dandelion
- Echinacea
- Elder
- Fennel
- Garlic
- Ginger
- Goldenseal
- Hawthorn
- Lavender
- Lemon balm
- Licorice
- Marshmallow

- Mullein
- Nettle
- Oats
- Peppermint
- Plantain
- Red clover
- Rosemary
- Sage
- Spearmint
- St.-John's-wort
- Thyme
- Turmeric
- Valerian
- Yarrow

Essential oils are another very useful application when creating these recipes. I use a high-quality, food-grade, non-GMO essential oil. Not only are you getting a fragrant smell that helps mask the odor of the cannabis, but you are also getting additional nutrients for your immune system. If you don't have the actual herb itself, essential oils can be extremely useful for supplementing missing ingredients for many applications.

# Recipes

As I have mentioned, once you have the cannabis extracted or infused, then it is very easy to include in any recipe. When making most baked goods, I like to use a one-to-one ratio of infused carrier to the plain carrier. For example, if a recipe calls for one cup of butter, then I use one-half cup of cannabis butter and one-half cup of plain butter. The same method is used for oils when baking. This helps to keep the overbearing taste and color to a minimum without sacrificing the medicinal qualities of the preparation.

I am including some of my tried-and-true recipes, but I encourage you to be inventive and customize these recipes as you see fit. I also encourage you to substitute ingredients that fit with a gluten-free, sugar-free, vegetarian, or vegan diet. Although I don't typically use boxed anything, I do understand that some people don't cook or bake from scratch. With that said, substituting the butter or oil specified in boxed recipes with cannabis-infused ingredients makes for easily created and dosed edibles.

Enjoy and green Blessings!

You can't have cancer if you have a functioning immune system and you
don't have a functioning immune system if you have cancer.
DR. RASHID BUTTAR, D.O., CENTER FOR ADVANCED MEDICINE, NC

Peter Hermes Furian/Shutterstock.com

# Edibles, Savory

# Compound Cannabis Butters

Compound cannabis butter is made by incorporating various spices and herbs into softened cannabis butter to use later in a dish. Adding a slice of this type of cannabis butter to a grilled steak or fish creates a lovely and healthy sauce. Use your imagination, or just spread on a piece of toast or biscuit.

For each recipe, start with 1 lb. softened cannabis-infused butter.

## Basil Cannabis Butter
Mince 2 oz. fresh basil and 2 oz. shallots. Add to softened cannabis butter with 2 tsp. lemon juice.

## Herb Cannabis Butter
Mince up to 1 cup of herbs such as parsley, dill, chives, tarragon, or chervil. Add to softened cannabis butter.

## Red Pepper Cannabis Butter
Puree 8 oz. roasted, peeled red bell peppers until liquid. Add to softened cannabis butter.

## Shallot Cannabis Butter
Blanch 8 oz. peeled shallots in boiling water. Dry and finely dice them, and mix with cannabis butter.

YuliiaHolovchenko/Shutterstock.com

# Cannabis Pesto Sauce

n this recipe, I will use the 1:1 ratio, as it lends itself well to this type of application. The original recipe called for 12 fl. oz. of olive oil, but I will use 10 oz. regular olive oil and 2 oz. cannabis-infused olive oil. This recipe is more flexible when setting up the controlled dosage.

The word "pesto" comes from Italy and means paste. Traditionally pesto is made with basil and pine nuts, but other herbs and nuts can be used. (I personally like using walnuts.) Try substituting other herbs like parsley, cilantro, carrot tops, or mint.

## Yield: 1½ pt.
### Ingredients

- 1¼ cup olive oil
- ¼ cup cannabis-infused olive oil
- ⅓ cup pine nuts or walnuts
- 5 oz. fresh basil leaves
- 1 oz. raw cannabis leaves
- 1 tbsp. garlic, chopped
- ½ cup Parmesan, grated
- ½ cup Romano, grated
- salt and pepper, to taste

### Directions

Place a third of the oil in a blender or food processor. Add all the remaining ingredients. Blend until smooth. Add the remaining oil, and blend a few more seconds to incorporate. You can also add 1 oz. sun-dried tomatoes for a nice variation. Use on pizza, pasta, or bread.

# Cannabis Hot Sauce

## Yield: 1 pt.
### Ingredients

- 20 Tabasco or serrano chilies, stemmed and cut crosswise into ⅛-inch slices, or 12 very ripe red jalapenos (about 10 oz.)
- 1½ tbsp. minced garlic
- ¾ cup thinly sliced onions
- ¾ tsp. salt
- 1 tsp. cannabis-infused avocado oil
- 2 cups water
- ½ cup distilled white vinegar
- ½ cup apple cider vinegar

## Directions

Combine the peppers, garlic, onions, salt, and cannabis-infused oil in a stainless-steel saucepan over high heat. Sauté for 3 minutes. Add the water and continue to cook, stirring occasionally, for about 20 minutes or until peppers are very soft and almost all of the liquid has evaporated. (This should be done in a very well-ventilated area!) Remove from heat and allow it to steep until mixture comes to room temperature. In a food processor, puree the mixture for 15 seconds or until smooth. With the food processor running, add the vinegar through the feed tube in a steady stream. Taste and season with more salt, if necessary. (This will depend on the heat level of the peppers you use, as well as the brand of vinegar used.) Strain the mixture through a stainless-steel fine mesh strainer, and then transfer to a sterilized pint jar or bottle and secure with an airtight lid. Refrigerate. Let age at least 2 weeks before using. Can be stored in the refrigerator for up to 6 months.

# Cannabis Chimichurri Sauce

Chimichurri is a fresh herb sauce originally from Argentina. This is traditionally served with grilled meats and works great as a marinade, too. Serve on pork, chicken, steak, or lamb kabobs.

## Yield: 1 pt.
### Ingredients

- ⅓ cup olive oil
- ⅓ cup cannabis-infused olive oil
- 8 garlic cloves, peeled
- ½ cup onion, chopped
- 2 tbsp. dried oregano, crushed
- 1½ fl. oz. fresh lemon juice
- 1 bunch fresh parsley
- 2 fl. oz. sherry wine vinegar
- 1 tsp. salt
- ½ tsp. crushed red pepper flakes
- ½ tsp. black pepper

## Directions
Combine all ingredients in a food processor and pulse until blended and slightly coarse in texture, not pureed.

HandmadePictures/Shutterstock.com

# Cannabis Mayonnaise

## Yield: 9 oz.
### Ingredients

- 1 egg yolk, pasteurized
- ½ tsp. fine salt
- ½ tsp. dry mustard
- 2 pinches sugar
- 2 tsp. freshly squeezed lemon juice
- 1 tbsp. white wine vinegar
- 1 cup cannabis-infused avocado oil

### Directions

In a glass bowl, whisk together egg yolk and dry ingredients. Combine lemon juice and vinegar in a separate bowl and then thoroughly whisk half into the yolk mixture. Start whisking briskly, and then start adding the oil a few drops at a time until the liquid seems to thicken and lighten a bit, which means you've got an emulsion on your hands. Once you reach that point, you can relax your arm a little (but just a little) and increase the oil flow to a constant (albeit thin) stream. Once half of the oil is in, add the rest of the lemon-juice mixture. Continue whisking until all of the oil is incorporated. Leave at room temperature for 1 to 2 hours. Refrigerate for up to 1 week.

Rimma Bondarenko/Shutterstock.com

# Cannabis Hollandaise Sauce

## Yield: 12 fl. oz.
**Ingredients**

- ¼ tsp. white peppercorns, crushed
- 1½ fl. oz. white wine vinegar
- 1 fl. oz. water
- 3 egg yolks, pasteurized
- ¾ fl. oz. lemon juice
- 8 oz. cannabis butter, warm
- salt and white pepper, to taste
- cayenne pepper, to taste

## Directions

Combine the peppercorns, vinegar, and water in a small saucepan, and reduce by one-half. Place the egg yolks in a stainless-steel bowl. Strain the vinegar and pepper reduction into the yolks. Place bowl over a double boiler, whipping the mixture continuously with a wire whisk. As the yolks cook, the mixture will thicken. When the mixture is thick enough to leave a trail across the surface when the whip is drawn away, remove the bowl from the double boiler. Do not overcook! Whip in half of the lemon juice to stop the yolks from cooking. Begin adding the cannabis butter a few drops at a time while consistently whipping until an emulsion starts to form. Once this has started, you can add the cannabis butter more quickly until all the cannabis butter is incorporated. Add the remaining lemon juice, and adjust the seasonings. Strain sauce through cheesecloth if lumpy. Serve immediately.

Ivonne Wierink/Shutterstock.com

# Cannabis Vinaigrette Dressing

## Yield: 1 pt.
### Ingredients

- 1 egg, pasteurized
- 1½ tsp. salt
- ¼ tsp. white pepper
- 1½ tsp. paprika
- 1½ tsp. dry mustard
- 1½ tsp. granulated sugar
- 1½ tsp. herbes de Provence
- 1 tsp. fresh cannabis leaves, chopped
- cayenne pepper, to taste
- 2 fl. oz. apple cider vinegar
- 6 fl. oz. cannabis-infused avocado oil
- 6 fl. oz. avocado oil
- 1½ fl. oz. lemon juice

### Directions

Place egg in a glass blender and whip at high speed until frothy. Add the dry ingredients and 1 fl. oz. vinegar to the eggs, continuing to whip until combined. While whipping at high speed, begin slowly adding oil in a steady stream until all oil has been incorporated and mixture emulsifies. If mixture gets too thick, add some of the vinegar and lemon juice until all of the oil has been added. Adjust consistency and seasoning to your liking.

# Cannabis–Raspberry Vinaigrette

## Yield: 1 pt.
### Ingredients

- ½ cup fresh or frozen raspberries
- 2 tbsp. lemon juice
- 2 tbsp. red wine vinegar
- 1 tsp. sugar
- 1 tsp. fresh cannabis leaves, chopped
- pinch of salt
- ¼ cup cannabis-infused avocado oil

### Directions
Place raspberries in a bowl and crush with a fork. Mix remaining ingredients together well and chill for a couple of hours. Stir well before serving.

# Cannabis Aioli

## Yield: 6 oz. or ¾ cup
**Ingredients**

- 3 garlic cloves, chopped
- 1 large egg, pasteurized
- 1 tbsp. freshly squeezed lemon juice
- 1 tbsp. fresh parsley, chopped
- 1 tbsp. fresh cannabis leaves, chopped
- ¼ cup olive oil
- ¼ cup cannabis-infused olive oil
- ½ tsp. salt
- ¼ freshly ground black pepper

## Directions

Combine the garlic, egg, lemon juice, parsley, salt, and pepper in a food processor or blender and puree. Combine oils and add in a slow stream. Continue to process until the mixture has formed a thick emulsion like mayonnaise.

Serve as you would mayonnaise. It is a great dipping sauce for many fried and baked foods.

Brent Hofacker/Shutterstock.com

# Cannabis Croutons

## Yield: approximately 2 pounds
### Ingredients

- ¾ cup cannabis butter
- 1 tbsp. garlic, chopped
- 1½ lb. French or sourdough bread cubes
- 2 tbsp. Parmesan cheese, grated
- 2 tsp. basil, dried
- 2 tsp. oregano, dried

## Directions

Preheat oven to 350°. In a saucepan, melt cannabis butter, and then add garlic and cook low and slow for 5 minutes. Toss the bread cubes with the cheese, basil, and oregano. Pour melted garlic cannabis butter over cubes and toss to coat evenly. Spread prepared bread cubes on a sheet pan in a single layer, and bake for approximately 15 minutes. Serve with salads, soups, and so on.

# Cannabis Wiener Schnitzel

Wiener schnitzel is a very thin, breaded, pan-fried cutlet made from veal. It is one of the best-known specialties of Viennese cuisine. The Wiener schnitzel is the national dish of Austria. This, along with the spätzle below, is one of my favorite dishes to make. It is also very tasty as a leftover. You can use other cuts of meat, like pork or chicken. Look for thin cuts at your local grocer to minimize the work required to pound cutlets very thin.

## Yield: 2 to 4 cutlets
### Ingredients

- 2 to 4 veal or pork cutlets
- 1 egg
- ½ cup flour
- 1 cup panko bread crumbs
- Salt and pepper, to taste
- 2 cups cannabis-infused coconut oil (for frying)

## Directions

Begin by preparing three bowls. Fill one bowl with flour, one with egg, and one with bread crumbs. Season the bowls with salt and pepper. Place cutlets on a sturdy surface and pound with a meat mallet until twice the original size. Cutlets should be quite thin. Place each pounded cutlet into the flour mixture and coat evenly. Pat off all excess flour. You want to just lightly coat the cutlet so that the egg will stick to it. Next place the flour-coated cutlet into the egg mixture. Again, let most of the egg drip back into the bowl. You want just a light egg coating, enough so that the bread crumbs will stick to the cutlet. Finally, place the egg-coated cutlet into the bread crumbs. Press hard to force the bread crumbs to coat the cutlet. Continue until cutlet is dry and not sticky. Set aside and prepare remaining cutlets. At this point, you could freeze for later use or proceed with frying.

For frying, pour the cannabis-infused coconut oil into a large frying pan and heat to 350°. Place cutlets in hot oil and fry until golden brown. Drain on paper towels. Keep warm in the oven until ready to serve. Nice traditional side dishes to serve with this dish are pickled red cabbage and the following spätzle recipe.

Brent Hofacker/Shutterstock.com

# Cannabis Spätzle

## Yield: 2 to 4 servings
**Ingredients**

- 2 eggs
- 6 fl. oz. water
- 8 oz. flour
- ¼ tsp. salt
- Pinch of nutmeg
- 1½ oz. cannabis butter
- salt and white pepper, to taste
- fresh parsley and cannabis leaves, chopped, for garnish

## Directions

Whisk eggs to blend. Add the water, flour, salt, and nutmeg. Mix by hand until blended. Batter should be smooth and gooey. Cover and refrigerate for approximately 30 minutes. Place batter into a colander suspended over a pot of boiling water. Work the batter through the colander's holes using a bowl scraper or spatula. The batter will drop into the boiling water. Lower the temperature to a simmer. When dumplings float to the top of the water, remove them and place them in an ice bath to stop the cooking. Once ready to serve, toss dumplings in cannabis butter and sauté until warm. Season with salt and white pepper. Garnish with chopped fresh cannabis and parsley leaves.

# Baked Pineapple and Cannabis

This goes well with ham or turkey. It is traditionally served at Thanksgiving but is tasty anytime.

## Yield: 6 servings
### Ingredients

- 20 oz. can pineapple chunks, drained
- 3 tbsp. pineapple juice
- ¾ cup sugar
- 3 tbsp. flour
- 1 cup cheddar cheese, shredded
- 1½ cup Ritz Crackers, crushed
- ¼ cup cannabis butter, melted

### Directions
Grease a small baking dish. Place drained pineapple in a bowl. Mix together the flour and sugar and pour over pineapple, mixing it together. Add the pineapple juice and shredded cheese and mix. Pour the mixture into baking dish. In a separate bowl, mix the Ritz Crackers with cannabis butter to create a coarse crumb. Sprinkle this mixture over pineapple mixture. Bake at 350° for approximately 15 to 20 minutes.

# Rosemary and Garlic Focaccia (Roman Flatbread with Cannabis)

## Yield: 1 half-sheet pan, 12 by 18 inches
### Ingredients

- 1 tbsp. granulated sugar
- 1 tbsp. active dry yeast
- 12 fl. oz. water, lukewarm
- 1 lb. 2 oz. all-purpose flour
- 2 tsp. kosher salt
- 3 oz. onion, chopped fine
- 3 tbsp. cannabis-infused olive oil
- 2 tbsp. fresh rosemary, crushed

## Directions
Combine the sugar, yeast, and water. Stir to dissolve the yeast. Stir in the flour, 4 ounces at a time. Stir in 1½ tsp. of the salt and onion. Mix well, and then knead on a lightly floured board or in the bowl of a mixer fitted with a dough hook until smooth. Place dough in an oiled bowl, cover, and let it ferment until doubled in size. Then punch down the dough and flatten it onto an oiled sheet pan, no more than an inch thick. Brush the top of the dough with cannabis-infused olive oil, and let it proof again until doubled in size. Sprinkle rosemary and the remaining salt on top of the dough. Bake at 400° until lightly browned, approximately 20 minutes.

# Sausage and Cannabis Soufflé

## Yield: 6 servings
**Ingredients**

- 12 eggs
- 1 cup cannabis-infused milk
- 3 cups whole milk
- 4 slices day-old bread
- 2 tsp. salt
- 2 tsp. dry mustard
- 2 lbs. sausage
- 2 cups cheddar cheese, grated

## Directions
Brown and drain sausage. Set it aside. In a bowl, beat eggs, salt, and mustard until incorporated. Add milk and bread, and gently mix. Add cheese and sausage. Pour mixture into a greased baking dish. Refrigerate overnight. Bake at 375° for 45 minutes. Let stand a few minutes before serving.

**Tip:** To reduce the risk of food-borne illness, it is recommended you use only fresh, properly refrigerated, clean grade A or AA eggs with intact shells, and avoid contact between the yolks or whites and the shell. Recipes that call for eggs that are raw or undercooked when the dish is served, use eggs that have been treated to destroy salmonella, by pasteurization or another approved method.

Anna Hoychuk/Shutterstock.com

# Sweet and Spicy Spacy Nuts

## Yield: 4 cups
**Ingredients**

- ½ tsp. ground cumin
- ½ tsp. cayenne pepper
- ½ tsp. ground cinnamon
- 4 cups unsalted mixed nuts (walnuts, pecans, almonds, etc.)
- 4 tbsp. cannabis butter
- 6 tbsp. brown sugar
- 1 tsp. salt

## Directions

Mix spices and set aside. Heat the nuts in a dry skillet and cook, stirring frequently, until they begin to toast, about 4 minutes. Add the cannabis butter and cook, stirring, until the nuts begin to darken, about 1 minute. Add the spices, the sugar, 1 tbsp. water, and the salt. Cook, stirring, until the sauce thickens and the nuts are glazed, about 5 minutes.

Remove the nuts from the heat and transfer to a baking sheet lined with aluminum foil, separating them with a fork. Let the nuts stand until cooled and the sugar has hardened, about 10 minutes. Store in an airtight container.

# Spiced Cannabis Pecans

**Yield: 1 cup**
**Ingredients**

- 1 tbsp. cannabis butter, soft
- ⅛ tsp. cayenne pepper
- ⅛ tsp. cinnamon
- ½ tsp. salt
- 1 tbsp. Worcestershire sauce
- 1 to 2 drops hot sauce
- 8 oz. pecan halves and pieces

**Directions**

Preheat oven to 300°. Combine all ingredients and blend well. Spread nuts on baking sheet and bake for 10 minutes. Toss and continue to bake for an additional 5 to 10 minutes. Remove from oven and allow to cool.

# Dizzy Chex Mix

**Yield: 10 cups**
**Ingredients**

- 5 cups crispy cereal
- 5 cups cheese crackers
- 3 tbsp. cannabis butter, melted
- ¼ tsp. garlic salt
- ¼ tsp. onion salt
- 2 tsp. lemon juice
- 4 tsp. Worcestershire sauce

**Directions**

Preheat oven to 250°. Combine cereal and crackers in a 13-by-9-by-2-inch baking sheet and set aside. Stir together cannabis butter and remaining ingredients. Stir cannabis-butter mixture over cereal and crackers. Toss to evenly distribute. Bake for 45 minutes, stirring every 15 minutes. Remove from oven and spread out on paper towels to cool. Store in airtight container.

# Dizzy Onion Chex Mix

## Yield: 10 cups
### Ingredients

- 1 package dry onion soup mix
- 3 tbsp. dry cultured powdered buttermilk
- 2 tbsp. dried chives
- 8 cups crispy cereal
- 2 cups pretzel sticks
- 3 tbsp. cannabis oil

### Directions

Combine onion soup mix, powdered buttermilk, and chives. Set aside. In a 2-gallon plastic bag, combine the cereal and pretzels. Pour oil over cereal mixture. Close bag and toss gently until well coated. Add the onion mixture and toss until well coated. Store in airtight container.

# Dizzy and Sweet Chex Mix

## Yield: 12 cups
### Ingredients

- 1 cup semisweet chocolate chips
- 1 tbsp. cannabis vanilla
- ¼ cup peanut butter
- ½ cup peanuts or other nuts (optional)
- 6 cups crispy cereal
- 1 cup powdered sugar

### Directions

In a large microwave-safe plastic bowl, microwave chocolate chips in 10-second intervals, stirring each time until chips are completely melted. Stir in peanut butter, peanuts, and vanilla. Stir to combine, and then add the crispy cereal and coat completely. Place powdered sugar in a 2-gallon plastic bag. Add the cereal mixture and gently toss until pieces are coated with the powdered sugar. Store in airtight container.

vsl/Shutterstock.com

# Cannabis Herbed Rice

## Yield: 4 to 6 servings
**Ingredients**

- 1 tbsp. cannabis butter
- 3 to 4 scallions, sliced thinly
- 2 cups long-grain rice
- 1 tsp. salt
- ½ tsp. freshly ground black pepper
- ¼ cup chopped fresh parsley
- 1 tbsp. cannabis spice, optional
- ½ tsp. lemon zest, optional

## Directions
Heat the cannabis butter in a medium saucepan over medium heat. Add the scallions and sauté for 2 to 3 minutes. Add the rice and stir until the rice is fully coated with cannabis butter.

Add 3 cups water and bring to a boil. Add the salt and pepper. Cover and reduce the heat to a simmer. Cook until the liquid is absorbed and the rice is al dente, 18 to 20 minutes.

Remove from heat. Fluff the rice with a fork, and stir in parsley, cannabis spice, and lemon zest, if using.

Creative Family/Shutterstock.com

# Edibles, Sweet

# Dizzy Fudge

This may be a sticker for some, but this recipe turns out so nicely if you use a low-wattage microwave. It can be made in a double boiler as well, but that is more difficult. I prefer to use the microwave for this recipe and for melting chocolate.

## Yield: 5 lbs.
### Ingredients

- 6 oz. cannabis butter
- 3 cups sugar
- ⅔ cups evaporated milk
- 12 oz. semisweet chocolate chips
- 7 oz. marshmallow cream
- 1 cup walnuts, chopped (optional)
- 1 tsp. vanilla

### Directions

Place cannabis butter in a microwave-safe bowl. Heat until just melted. Add sugar and milk; mix well. Microwave on high 3 minutes. Remove from microwave and stir well. Replace bowl in microwave and cook on high for 2 minutes, removing to stir well. Repeat this step two more times. (Stirring between intervals is key to a smooth finish. You may need to adjust cooking time depending on your microwave. Again, you are looking for a smooth and creamy finish.) Remove from microwave and add the chocolate chips to the hot mixture; then add the marshmallow cream, vanilla, and nuts. Use a hand blender to mix all together, scraping the bowl to incorporate all ingredients. Pour mixture in a pan and let cool to room temperature. Cut final candy into 1-by-1-inch squares.

# Dizzy Caramels

## Yield: 4 lbs.
### Ingredients

- 1 cup sugar
- 1 cup cannabis butter
- 1 cup dark corn syrup
- 14 oz. sweetened condensed milk
- 1 tsp. vanilla

### Directions

Line an 8-inch square pan with foil. Butter the foil and set aside. In a pot, bring sugar, corn syrup, and cannabis butter to boil over medium heat, stirring constantly. Reduce heat slightly, and let the mixture slowly boil for 4 minutes without stirring. Remove from heat and stir in milk. Place candy thermometer into pot. Return pot to heat and cook until mixture reaches the soft ball stage (238°), which should take approximately 30 minutes. Remove from heat and stir in vanilla. Pour into prepared pan to cool. Cut into 1-by-1-inch pieces.

# Sweet 'n' Salty No-Bake Cannabis Peanut Butter Bars

## Yield: 12 bars
### Ingredients

- 6 tbsp. cannabis butter, melted
- ½ tsp. pure vanilla extract
- 4 oz. pretzel sticks, crushed (about 1 cup of crumbs)
- ⅔ cup creamy peanut butter
- 1 cup powdered sugar, sifted
- ¾ cup bittersweet chocolate chips
- 3 tbsp. creamy peanut butter

## Directions

Line an 8-by-8-inch pan with aluminum foil or parchment paper and set aside. In a large bowl, stir together cannabis butter and vanilla extract. With an electric mixer on low speed, add in the pretzel crumbs, ⅔ cup peanut butter, and powdered sugar. Mix until thoroughly combined. Press mixture into prepared pan to form an even crust. In a medium microwave-safe bowl, place the chocolate chips and peanut butter. Microwave on medium power (50 percent) for 1 minute. Remove and stir. If chocolate is not melted, return to microwave and repeat heating step, stirring every 10 seconds to avoid scorching. Stir until smooth. Using an offset spatula, spread chocolate mixture over the prepared crust. Refrigerate bars for at least one hour.

Irina Meliukh/Shutterstock.com

# Salted Caramel Sauce

**Yield: 1 ½ cup**
**Ingredients**

- 1 packed cup brown sugar
- ½ cup half-and-half
- 4 tbsp. cannabis butter
- 1 tsp. salt
- 1 tbsp. vanilla extract

**Directions**

Mix the brown sugar, half-and-half, cannabis butter, and salt in a saucepan over medium to low heat. Cook while whisking gently for 5 to 7 minutes, until mixture gets thicker. Add the vanilla and cook another minute to thicken further. Turn off the heat. Let it cool slightly, and pour the sauce into a jar. Refrigerate until cold.

271 EAK MOTO/Shutterstock.com

# Cannabis Chocolate Drops

## Yield: 9 oz.
### Ingredients

- 8 oz. high-quality dark-chocolate chips
- 1 oz. cannabis butter

### Directions

Place chips and cannabis butter in a microwave-safe plastic bowl. Slowly heat chocolate in 10-second increments, stirring each time. Mixture will look like it is not melting, but it is. Keep cooking as stated above until mixture is smooth and silky. Pour into molds and place into refrigerator to set.

Foodio/Shutterstock.com

# Pot Brownies

## Yield: 9 servings
**Ingredients**

- Nonstick vegetable oil spray
- ½ cup (1 stick) cannabis butter, cut into 1-inch pieces
- 1¼ cups sugar
- ¾ cup natural unsweetened cocoa powder
- ½ tsp. kosher salt
- 1 tsp. vanilla extract
- 2 large eggs
- ⅓ cup all-purpose flour

## Directions

Preheat oven to 325°. Line an 8-by-8-by-2-inch glass baking dish with foil, pressing firmly into pan and leaving a 2-inch overhang. Coat foil with nonstick spray; set baking dish aside.

Melt cannabis butter in a small saucepan over medium heat. Let cool slightly. Whisk sugar, cocoa, and salt in a medium bowl to combine. Pour cannabis butter in a steady stream into dry ingredients, whisking constantly to blend. Whisk in vanilla. Add eggs one at a time, beating vigorously to blend after each addition. Add flour and stir until just combined (do not overmix). Scrape batter into prepared pan and smooth top. Bake until top begins to crack and a toothpick inserted into the center comes out with a few moist crumbs attached, 25 to 30 minutes.

Transfer the pan to a wire rack, and let the brownies cool completely in the pan. If desired, ice cool brownies with Ganja Ganache. Using the foil overhang, lift the brownies out of the pan and transfer them to a cutting board. Cut into 16 squares.

Chachamp/Shutterstock.com

# Double Chocolate Chip and Cannabis Cookies

## Yield: 24 cookies
### Ingredients

- 12 oz. semisweet chocolate chips
- 10 oz. dark chocolate chips (60 percent cacao)
- 6 tbsp. cannabis butter
- 3 eggs
- 1 cup sugar
- ⅓ cup all-purpose flour
- ½ tsp. baking powder
- 1 cup chopped walnuts

## Directions

In double boiler over hot water, melt bittersweet chocolate chips and cannabis butter. In large bowl with electric mixer or whisk, beat eggs and sugar until thick. Stir eggs and sugar into chocolate mixture. In small bowl, stir together flour and baking powder, and then stir into chocolate mixture. Gently mix in chocolate chips and walnuts. Using a sheet of plastic wrap, form dough into two logs, each 2 inches in diameter and about 12 inches long. As dough will be quite soft, use plastic wrap to hold dough in log shape. Wrap tightly; refrigerate at least 1 hour or until firm.

Heat oven to 375°. Unwrap dough; with sharp knife, cut it into ¾-inch slices. Place slices 1 ½ inches apart on greased or parchment-lined cookie sheet. Bake 12 to 14 minutes or until a shiny crust forms on top but the interior is still soft. Cool on baking sheet; store in airtight tin up to 1 week.

Africa Studio/Shutterstock.com

# Double Chocolate and Cannabis Cupcakes

## Yield: 12 cupcakes
### Ingredients

- 1¼ cups all-purpose flour
- 2 tsp. baking powder
- ⅓ cup cocoa powder
- 1 cup sugar
- ½ tsp. salt
- 7 tbsp. cannabis butter, softened
- 3 large eggs, room temperature
- ⅔ cup milk
- 1 tbsp. sour cream or Greek yogurt
- 1 tsp. pure vanilla extract

### Directions

Preheat the oven to 350°. Sift the flour, baking soda, and cocoa into a bowl. Add the sugar, salt, and cannabis butter. Mix until it resembles fine bread crumbs. In a separate bowl, whisk the eggs, milk, vanilla extract, and sour cream (or yogurt) together until well blended.

Slowly pour in the egg mixture to combine. Mix gently until smooth. Line cupcake pan with paper liners, and spoon mixture into the liners, filling only half full.

Bake for 20 minutes until firm and springy to the touch. Transfer slightly cooled cupcakes to a wire rack to cool completely. Frost cupcakes with Chocolate Cannabis Buttercream.

# Chocolate Cannabis Buttercream Frosting

This recipe makes enough buttercream to frost about 12 to 15 cupcakes. Double this recipe to frost an 8- or 9-inch two-layer cake. Frosting can be made ahead and refrigerated. To use, let frosting come to room temperature and beat until light and fluffy. Frosting will keep in refrigerator for 1 week.

## Yield: 3 cups
### Ingredients

- 3 cups powdered sugar, sifted
- ½ cup cocoa powder, sifted
- 8 oz. cannabis butter, room temperature
- ¼ tsp. fine salt
- 2 tsp. pure vanilla extract
- 1 to 2 tbsp. heavy or whipping cream

## Directions

In the bowl of a stand mixer fitted with the paddle attachment, mix together the sugar and cannabis butter. Mix on low speed until well blended, and then increase the speed to medium and beat for another 3 minutes. Add the salt, vanilla, and cream, and beat on medium for 1 minute, adding more cream if needed. Once you have the consistency as you like, beat on medium high for another 5 minutes, until light and fluffy.

# Cannabis Gingersnaps

## Yield: 36 cookies
### Ingredients

- ¾ cup cannabis-infused shortening
- 2 cups sugar, divided
- ¼ cup molasses
- 1 egg
- 2 cups all-purpose flour
- ¼ tsp. salt
- 2 tsp. baking soda
- 1 tsp. cloves
- 1 tsp. cinnamon
- 1 tsp. ginger

## Directions
Preheat oven to 350°. Cream cannabis-infused shortening and 1 cup sugar in a large mixing bowl. Add molasses and egg. Mix well. Sift dry ingredients together. Add to shortening mixture. Roll into balls. Roll in sugar and place on cookie sheet. Bake for 10 minutes.

Anna Hoychuk/Shutterstock.com

# Cannabis Lemon Bars

## Yield: 9 to 12 bars
### Ingredients—Crust

- 2 cups all-purpose flour, sifted
- ½ cup powdered sugar, sifted
- ½ cup cold cannabis butter
- ½ cup cold unsalted butter

### Directions

Preheat oven to 350°. Lightly grease a 13-by-9-by-2-inch baking pan. In a bowl, sift flour and sugar together. Cut in the butters until the mixture looks like sand. Press mixture into prepared pan. Bake for 20 to 25 minutes or until lightly browned.

### Ingredients—Lemon Filling

- 4 slightly beaten eggs
- 2 cups sugar
- ¼ cup all-purpose flour
- ⅓ cup lemon juice
- ½ tsp. baking powder

### Directions

Preheat oven to 350°. Beat together eggs. Gradually add sugar and lemon juice. Sift flour and baking powder and stir into egg mixture. Pour into baked crust. Bake for 25 minutes. Cool, and then chill in refrigerator several hours or overnight. Sprinkle with powdered sugar.

# Apple Raspberry Cannabis Bars

**Yield: 12 bars**
**Ingredients**

- 1 cup cannabis butter, at room temperature, plus more for the pan
- 2½ cups all-purpose flour
- 1½ tsp. baking soda
- ¾ tsp. kosher salt
- ½ cup packed light-brown or dark-brown sugar
- 1 large egg
- ½ cup old-fashioned rolled oats
- 4 small apples, peeled, cored, and chopped (about 2½ cups)
- 2 cups frozen raspberries
- ½ cup granulated sugar
- 2 tsp. cornstarch

## Directions

Preheat the oven to 350°. Butter a 9-inch-square baking pan and line it with parchment paper, leaving a 2-inch overhang on two sides. In a large bowl, whisk together the flour, baking soda, and salt. In a medium bowl, beat the cannabis butter and the brown sugar with an electric mixer on medium speed until fluffy, about 2 minutes. Beat in the egg. Spread about two-thirds of the batter evenly over the bottom of the prepared pan with an offset spatula. Bake the bottom crust until it is golden brown, 24 to 26 minutes. Mix the remaining batter with the oats and set aside.

Meanwhile, in a medium saucepan, combine the apples, raspberries, and sugar, and cook over medium heat, stirring occasionally, until the mixture is bubbling and the fruit has broken down, 5 to 6 minutes. In a small bowl, mix about 3 tbsp. of the fruit mixture with the cornstarch until smooth. Add the cornstarch mixture to the fruit and simmer for another 2 to 3 minutes. Remove the jam from the heat and let cool slightly.

Top the bottom crust with the fruit and spread it out evenly. Top the fruit with the oat-crumb mixture, squeezing it to make some larger clumps. Bake until the top is golden brown, 28 to 32 minutes. Transfer the pan to a rack to cool completely. Using the parchment, lift out the entire bar mixture and place it on a cutting board. Cut into squares.

# Cranberry Orange Cannabis Cake Bites

**Yield: 24 petite cakes**

**Ingredients**

- 1 cup all-purpose flour
- 1 tsp. baking powder
- ¼ tsp. salt
- 4 tbsp. cannabis butter, softened
- ½ cup sugar
- 1 egg
- 1 tbsp. finely grated orange zest
- ½ cup milk
- ⅓ cup sweetened dried cranberries, coarsely chopped

**Directions**

Preheat oven to 325°. Lightly grease pan. In a small bowl, stir together flour, baking powder, and salt. In large bowl, beat cannabis butter and sugar with electric mixer until light and fluffy. Add egg and orange zest, and beat until well combined. Add flour mixture in three additions, alternating with milk. Add cranberries and beat until just combined. Bake 11 to 13 minutes or until a toothpick inserted in the cake comes out clean. Cool in the pan for 5 minutes. Remove to wire racks to cool completely.

# Cannabis Sunshine Muffins

**Yield: 18 large muffins**
**Ingredients**

- 2 cups all-purpose flour
- 2¼ cups sugar
- 4 tsp. baking soda
- 1 tbsp. salt
- 4 tsp. cinnamon, ground
- 1¾ cup carrots, grated
- ¾ cup raisins
- ½ cup pecan pieces
- ½ cup coconut, shredded
- ¾ cup apple, unpeeled, grated
- 6 eggs
- 10½ fl. oz. cannabis oil
- 4 tsp. vanilla extract

**Directions**

Preheat oven to 350°. Sift the dry ingredients together and set aside. Combine the carrots, raisins, pecans, coconut, and apple. Whisk together the eggs, oil, and vanilla extract. Toss the carrot mixture into the dry ingredients. Then add the liquid ingredients, stirring just until incorporated. Bake in a well-greased or lined muffin pan for approximately 25 minutes.

MSPhotographic/Shutterstock.com

# Cannabis Pecan Pie

## Yield: 8 servings
**Ingredients**

- 3 eggs, slightly beaten
- ¾ cup sugar
- 1 cup dark non-GMO corn syrup
- 1 cup pecan pieces (or whole pecans)
- 4 tbsp. cannabis butter
- 1 tsp. vanilla
- 1 unbaked 9-inch pie shell (see the recipe for pie dough)

## Directions

Preheat oven to 350°. Boil sugar and syrup together slowly (about 2 to 3 minutes). Pour slowly into slightly beaten eggs. Stir in cannabis butter, vanilla, and nuts.

Let mixture cool to room temperature before pouring into uncooked pastry shell. Bake for 50 to 60 minutes. Do not overcook.

# Basic Cannabis Pie Dough

## Yield: 9-inch pie shell
### Ingredients

- 1¼ cups all-purpose flour
- 1 tbsp. sugar
- ¼ tsp. salt
- ½ cup cold cannabis butter, cut into ¼-inch cubes
- 3 tbsp. very cold water

## Directions

To make the dough by hand, in a large bowl, stir together the flour, sugar, and salt. Using a pastry cutter or a couple of knives, cut the cannabis butter into the flour mixture until the texture resembles coarse cornmeal, with pieces of cannabis butter no larger than small peas. Add the water, and mix with a fork just until the dough pulls together.

Transfer the dough to a work surface, pat into a ball, and flatten into a disk. (Although many dough recipes call for chilling the dough at this point, this dough should be rolled out immediately for best results.) Lightly flour the work surface, and then flatten the disk with 6 to 8 gentle taps of the rolling pin. Lift the dough and give it a quarter turn. Lightly dust the top of the dough or the rolling pin with flour as needed, and then roll it out into a round at least 12 inches in diameter and about ⅛ inch thick. Makes enough dough for one 9-inch single crust.

# Canna Banana Bread

## Yield: 1 loaf, 8 to 10 slices
### Ingredients

- 1⅔ cups all-purpose flour
- 1 tsp. baking soda
- ¼ tsp. ground cinnamon
- ½ tsp. salt
- 1 cup plus 2 tbsp. sugar
- 2 eggs
- ½ cup cannabis-infused oil (coconut or avocado is better)
- 3½ bananas, very ripe, mashed
- 2 tbsp. crème fraiche or sour cream
- 1 tsp. vanilla
- ⅔ cup walnuts, toasted and chopped

### Directions

Preheat oven to 350°. Line bottom of a one-pound loaf pan with parchment paper.

Sift together the flour, baking soda, cinnamon, and salt. Beat sugar and eggs with a whisk until light and fluffy, about 10 minutes. Drizzle in oil. Add mashed bananas, crème fraiche, and vanilla. Fold in dry ingredients and nuts. Pour into lined loaf pan, and bake for 45 minutes to 1 hour.

Note: My oven bakes this at exactly 1 hour. If you open the oven before the bread is set, it will fall. You may have to bake one to see how it works with your oven.

# Dizzy Monkey Bread

## Yield: 10 to 12 servings
### Ingredients

- ¾ cup sugar
- 2 tsp. cinnamon, divided
- 4 cans of biscuits, cut into fourths
- 1 cup brown sugar
- 1 tbsp. maple syrup
- ½ cup cannabis-infused butter

## Directions

Preheat oven to 350°. Mix sugar and 1 tsp. cinnamon in a ziplock bag. Place several biscuit pieces into the sugar/cinnamon mixture and coat each piece evenly until all pieces are coated. Put biscuit pieces in a Bundt pan, pressing gently if needed to fit into pan. Mix brown sugar, syrup, the remaining cinnamon, and the cannabis butter in a small saucepan and bring to a boil. Pour mixture over biscuits. Bake 30 to 40 minutes.

# Cannabis Pine Bark

## Yield: 50 squares
### Ingredients

- 35 saltine crackers
- 1 cup cannabis butter
- 1 cup light-brown sugar, packed
- ½ tsp. almond or vanilla extract
- 5 (4 oz.) chocolate bars, chopped

### Directions

Preheat oven to 400°. Line a 15-by-10-by-1-inch sheet pan with foil. Lightly spray with nonstick cooking spray.

Place saltine crackers salty side up in the pan. In a saucepan, boil cannabis butter and sugar 2 to 3 minutes, stirring constantly. Remove from heat and stir in extract. Pour mixture slowly over crackers to cover completely, and bake for 4 to 6 minutes until bubbly. Remove from oven. Top with chocolate and spread as chocolate begins to melt. Cool slightly, and then transfer to cutting board to cool completely. Cut into 1-by-1-inch pieces.

Wollertz/Shutterstock.com

# Cannabis Chocolate-Dipped Strawberries

## Yield: about 20 strawberries
### Ingredients

- 6 oz. semisweet chocolate, chopped
- 1 oz. cannabis-infused butter
- 3 oz. white chocolate, chopped
- 1 lb. strawberries with stems, washed and dried very well

## Directions

Place the semisweet and white chocolates into separate heatproof medium bowls. Fill 2 medium saucepans with 2 inches of water and bring to a simmer over medium heat. Turn off the heat; set the bowls of chocolate over the water to melt. Stir until smooth. (Alternatively, melt the chocolates in a microwave at half power for 15-second intervals, stir, and then heat for another 15 seconds until completely melted.)

Once the chocolates are melted and smooth, remove from heat. Line a sheet pan with parchment or waxed paper. Holding the strawberry by the stem, dip the fruit into the dark chocolate, lift, and twist slightly, letting any excess chocolate fall back into the bowl. Set strawberries on the parchment paper. Repeat with the rest of the strawberries. Dip a fork in the white chocolate and drizzle the white chocolate over the dipped strawberries.

Set the strawberries aside until the chocolate sets, about 30 minutes.

Viktory Panchenko/Shutterstock.com

# Cannabis Marshmallow Treats

## Yield: 24 2-inch squares
### Ingredients

- 3 tbsp. cannabis butter
- 4 cups minimarshmallows
- 6 cups rice cereal (plain, chocolate, or rainbow)

### Directions

Melt cannabis butter in large saucepan over low heat. Add marshmallows and stir until melted. Remove from heat. Add cereal and stir until completely coated. Using a buttered spatula, press mixture evenly into a 13-by-9-by-2-inch pan coated with cooking spray. Cut into 2-inch squares once cool.

### Options

Dip squares into cannabis-infused chocolate, nuts, or sprinkles, or add lollipop sticks for easy eating.

# Oatmeal Raisin and Cannabis Cookies

## Yield: about 48 cookies
### Ingredients

- 1 cup cannabis butter
- 1 cup brown sugar, packed
- ½ cup white sugar
- 2 eggs
- 1 tsp. vanilla
- 1½ cups all-purpose flour
- 1 tsp. baking soda
- 1 tsp. cinnamon
- ½ tsp. salt
- 3 cups uncooked oats (quick or old-fashioned)
- 1 cup raisins

## Directions

Preheat oven to 350°. Beat together cannabis butter and sugars until creamy. Add eggs one at a time, incorporating each one, and then add vanilla and beat well. Combine flour, soda, cinnamon, and salt, and add them to cannabis-butter mixture. Stir in oats and raisins, and mix well. Drop by rounded tablespoons onto parchment paper–lined cookie sheet. Bake 10 to 12 minutes or until golden brown.

# Canna Butter Cookies

## Yield: 30 to 40 cookies
### Ingredients

- 5 oz. cannabis butter, softened
- ½ cup sugar
- 1 large egg, room temperature
- 2 cups all-purpose flour

### Directions

Preheat oven to 350°. Put cannabis butter in mixer and beat until smooth. Add sugar and continue to beat until blended. Add egg and beat on low speed until incorporated. Add flour and mix gently; do not overmix. Transfer dough to a work surface, and knead until it just comes together. Divide dough in half, and shape each half into a 4-inch disk. Wrap with plastic and chill until firm, about 4 hours.

Line cookie sheets with parchment paper. Working with one disk at a time, roll dough on a lightly floured surface until it is approximately ⅛ to ¼ inch thick. Using a 1½-inch round cookie cutter, cut out as many shapes as you can, gathering the scraps to roll out again. Bake cookies 8 to 10 minutes or until set. These cookies will not take on a lot of color. Cool on a wire rack. These cookies can be iced if desired.

Hanabiyori/Shutterstock.com

# Cannabis Pound Cake

## Yield: 10 to 12 servings
**Ingredients**

- 1 cup cannabis butter
- 3 cups sugar
- 6 large eggs
- 3 cups flour, sifted, then measured
- ¼ tsp. baking soda
- ¼ tsp. salt
- 8 oz. sour cream
- 1 tsp. vanilla

## Directions

Preheat oven to 350°. Cream cannabis butter. Add sugar slowly to cream mixture together until light and fluffy. In a bowl, sift dry ingredients together. Add flour and eggs alternately, starting with flour and ending with flour. Add vanilla.

Grease and flour a lined tube or Bundt pan. Pour mixture into pan, and bake for 45 to 60 minutes, until toothpick comes out clean and sides of cake are pulling away from the pan. Do not overbake.

# Cannabis French Toast Strata

## Yield: 6 to 8 slices
### Ingredients

- 1 large loaf of French bread (day old is better)

## Batter

- 8 eggs
- 2 cups milk
- 1½ cups half-and-half
- 2 tsp. vanilla

## Sauce

- ¼ tsp. cinnamon
- ¾ cup cannabis butter
- 1⅓ cup brown sugar
- 3 tsp. light corn syrup

## Directions

Preheat oven to 350°. Spray casserole pan with nonstick cooking spray. Slice bread in pieces that will fit in the bottom of the casserole pan in one layer. Prepare batter by mixing all ingredients together until incorporated. Pour batter over French-bread slices in casserole dish. Cover and place in refrigerator overnight.

Remove from refrigerator and prepare the sauce. Mix sauce ingredients in a small saucepan, and heat until cannabis butter is melted and slightly bubbling. Do not overcook. Pour mixture over casserole. Cook uncovered for approximately 40 minutes. Allow to cool slightly and serve with fruit.

Africa Studio/Shutterstock.com

# Cannabis Jell-O

## Yield: about 2 cups
### Ingredients

- 1 packet Jell-O (sweetened, any flavor)
- 1 cup boiling water
- 4 oz. cannabis vodka or grain-alcohol cannabis tincture
- 4 oz. cold water

### Directions
Place Jell-O into a bowl. Pour boiling water over the powder and stir to dissolve. Make sure all of the powder has dissolved, and then add the tincture and mix well. Add the cold water and stir until mixed completely. Pour mixture into molds. Refrigerate until set.

# Cannabis–Vanilla Bean Ice Cream

## Yield: 1 quart
### Ingredients

- 1¼ cups whole milk
- 1¾ cups cannabis-infused heavy cream
- 1 vanilla bean, split (or 2 tsp. pure vanilla extract)
- ½ cup plus 2 tbsp. sugar
- ⅓ cup light corn syrup
- 6 large egg yolks

### Directions

Combine the milk, cream, and corn syrup in a heavy saucepan, stirring constantly until mixture comes just to a boil. Remove from heat. Add vanilla bean at this point, if using. In a separate bowl, whisk egg yolks and sugar together, and mix until light in color and smooth. Temper the egg mixture with one-third of the hot milk, and then pour the mixture back into the remaining milk mixture. Cook over medium heat, stirring constantly, until slightly thickened. Pour mixture through a fine-mesh strainer into a clean bowl, and stir in vanilla extract (if using) at this point. Chill the cooked ice-cream base completely in the refrigerator 24 hours before processing.

Pour mixture into ice-cream machine and process according to the manufacturer's instructions. Chill ice cream in airtight container.

There are many variations to this recipe. To make chocolate ice cream, add 6 oz. finely chopped high-quality chocolate to the hot mixture after straining. Stir until completely melted and mixed. You can also add marshmallows, cherries, fruit, cookies, and so on.

You can't have cancer if you have a functioning immune system and you
don't have a functioning immune system if you have cancer.
— DR. RASHID BUTTAR, D.O., CENTER FOR ADVANCED MEDICINE, NC

# Port-a-Pot Ganache

## Yield: about 2 cups
### Ingredients

- 18 oz. high-quality chocolate, finely chopped
- 1 cup cannabis-infused heavy cream
- ½ cup high-quality port
- 2 tbsp. cannabis butter
- 1 tsp. vanilla

## Directions

Heat chocolate, cream, and port in microwave-safe bowl in 1-minute increments, stirring after each minute, until the chocolate has melted and is smooth. Stir in the cannabis butter and vanilla. Cover and refrigerate until ready to use.

# Ganja Ganache

## Yield: about 2 cups
## Ingredients

- 8 oz. high-quality chocolate, finely chopped
- 8 oz. cannabis-infused heavy cream
- 2 tsp. cannabis butter
- 2 tsp. vanilla

## Directions

Place chocolate in a heatproof bowl. Heat cream in small saucepan until it just comes to a boil. Immediately pour hot cream over the chocolate and let set a few minutes. With a whisk, mix cream and chocolate together until it becomes smooth and silky. Add more or less cream to gain the desired consistency. This recipe is good for coating or filling cupcakes and such. Play around with it, and you'll find so many different applications.

# Cannabis Marshmallows

## Yield: about 30 to 40 small to medium marshmallows
**Ingredients**

- ¼ cup water
- ¼ cup light corn syrup
- ¾ cup sugar
- 2 egg whites
- 1 tbsp. gelatin
- 2 tbsp. cold water
- ¼ tsp. cannabis-infused vanilla extract

## Directions

Combine water, corn syrup, and sugar in a saucepan fitted with a candy thermometer. Bring to a boil, and continue to boil until candy thermometer reaches 235 degrees.

Meanwhile, whip the egg whites until soft peaks form. Sprinkle the gelatin over the water and set aside.

When the syrup reaches 235°, remove it from the heat, add the gelatin, and mix. Slowly pour the syrup into the whipped egg whites. Add the vanilla and continue whipping until stiff.

Cover a sheet pan with parchment paper, and then sprinkle it with powdered sugar. Pour the marshmallow onto the pan and spread it out. Let it cool about 2 hours. Then, with a pair of scissors or a cookie cutter dipped in cornstarch, cut out shapes.

# Cannabis Chantilly Cream

## Yield: 2 to 2½ quarts
### Ingredients

- 4 cups cannabis-infused heavy cream, chilled
- 3 oz. powdered sugar (optional)
- 2 tsp. vanilla or other flavoring

## Directions

Place cream in a chilled mixing bowl. Using a balloon whisk, whisk the cream until just slightly thickened. Add the sugar and vanilla, and continue whisking until you reach the desired consistency. Do not over whip. You will end up with a sweet cannabis butter. Mixture will keep in the refrigerator for several hours. If mixture deflates, you can whip it up again.

Volodymyr Krasyuk/Shutterstock.com

# Cannabis Lollipops

## Yield: 20 lollipops
### Ingredients

- ¾ cup granulated sugar
- ½ cup light corn syrup
- ¼ cup cannabis butter
- 3 oz. box of sweetened flavored gelatin (strawberry is my favorite)
- ¼ tsp. citric acid (if you want sour candies)

## Directions

Spray candy molds with nonstick cooking spray, and place lollipop sticks in them. In a saucepan, add the sugar, syrup, and cannabis butter. Mix together. Place candy thermometer in saucepan, stirring constantly, and bring saucepan to a boil. Once mixture has just started to boil, stop stirring and increase heat slightly. Continue boiling until mixture reaches 285°. Remove thermometer, and pour in the gelatin. Stir quickly, as mixture will want to set up. Quickly pour into candy molds, and allow to cool completely.

# Dinner and a Movie

I thought it would be a nice addition to this cookbook to put together an actual menu that you could prepare yourself. Then sit down with friends, enjoy the fruits of your labor, and watch the movie *Reefer Madness*. I hope you can appreciate absurdity of this movie and the way it brainwashed the good people of this earth.

Milligrams of cannabis consumed are listed by each dish. You can increase or decrease the milligrams as you wish. Bon appétit!

# MENU

### Fresh Garden Salad
*with fresh Cannabis-Raspberry Vinaigrette*
*made with approximately 2 milligrams of THC*

### Chimichurri Cannabis Kabobs
*served with Cannabis Herb Rice*
*made with approximately 10 milligrams of THC*

### French Bread
*with Cannabis Olive Oil and balsamic vinegar*
*made with approximately 1 milligram of THC*

### Vanilla Bean and Cannabis Ice Cream
*with Port-a-Pot Ganache, Cannabis Chantilly Cream, and chocolate sprinkles and a cherry on top*
*made with approximately 10 milligrams of THC*

### Coffee Pot
*with optional Cannabis-Infused Cream and sugar or honey*
*made with approximately 2 milligrams of THC*

*Total cannabis consumption for this meal is approximately 2 grams, or 25 milligrams.*

# RESOURCES

Americans for Safe Access. "Americans for Safe Access." www. safeaccessnow.org.

Bollinger, Ty. "The Truth About Cancer." www.thetruthaboutcancer.com.

Bulk Apothecary. "Bulk Apothecary." www.bulkapothecary.com.

Champlin, Frank, and Deborah Champlin. "Cannabis 420Edu: Dispelling the Myths About Cannabis." www.Cannabis420Edu.com.

Christopher, John R. "School of Natural Healing." www.snh.cc.

Drug Policy Alliance. "Drug Policy Alliance." www.drugpolicy.org.

Gallagher, John. "Learning Herbs." www.learningherbs.com.

Gladstar, Rosemary. "Sage Mountain." www.sagemountain.com.

Green Flower Media. "Green Flower." www.learngreenflower.com.

Green Med Info. "The Science of Natural Healing." www.greenmedinfo.com.

Herer, Jack. "The Emperor Wears No Clothes." www.jackherer.com.

Mechoulam, Raphael. "The Grandfather of Cannabis Research." www.mechoulamthescientist.com.

Melamede PhD, Dr. Robert. "Dr. Robert Melamede, PhD." www.drbobmelamede.com

Mountain Rose Herbs. "Mountain Rose Herbs." www.mountainroseherbs.com.

National Organization for the Reform of Marijuana Laws. "NORML: Working to Reform Marijuana Laws." www.norml.org.

National Restaurant Association Educational Foundation. "ServSafe Certification." www.servsafe.com.

Natural News. "Natural News." www.naturalnews.com.

Oaksterdam University. "Welcome to Oaksterdam University." www.oaksterdamuniversity.com.

Sulak, Dustin. "Healer.com" www.healer.com.

**COMMON EQUIVALENTS**

Here are some common equivalents and abbreviations that I found helpful when measuring and converting ounces, grams, teaspoons, tablespoons, and so on.

- ⅛ teaspoon = dash = pinch = smidge
- 3 teaspoons = 1 tablespoon = ½ fluid ounce
- 2 tablespoons = 6 teaspoons = 1 fluid ounce
- 4 tablespoons = ¼ cup = 2 fluid ounces
- 16 tablespoons = 1 cup = 8 fluid ounces
- 1 cup = ½ pound = ½ pint = 8 fluid ounces
- 2 cups = 1 pound = 1 pint = 16 fluid ounces
- 4 cups = 2 pounds = 2 pints = 1 quart = 32 fluid ounces
- 4 quarts = 1 gallon = 128 fluid ounces

## Abbreviations

- teaspoon = tsp.
- tablespoon = tbsp.
- cup = c.
- pint = pt.
- ounce = oz.
- pound = lb.
- gram = g
- milliliter = ml
- quart = qt.
- fluid ounce = fl. oz.

## Converting Grams and Ounces

To convert to grams or milliliters, multiply the number of ounces by 30:

$$8 \text{ oz.} \times 30 = 240 \text{ g}$$
$$8 \text{ fl. oz.} \times 30 = 240 \text{ ml}$$

To convert to ounces, divide the number of grams/milliliters by 30:

$$240 \text{ g} \div 30 = 8 \text{ oz.}$$
$$240 \text{ ml} \div 30 = 8 \text{ fl. oz.}$$

- 1 gram = 0.035 ounces = 1/30 (one-thirtieth) of an ounce
- 28.35 grams = 1 ounce (rounded to 30)
- 454 grams = 1 pound
- 2.2 pounds = about 1 kilogram
- 5 milliliters = 1 teaspoon
- 15 milliliters = 1 tablespoon
- 29.57 milliliters = 1 fluid ounce

## Other Helpful Tips

- The freezing point of water is 32° Fahrenheit.
- The boiling point of water is 212° Fahrenheit.
- The boiling point of alcohol is 173.1° Fahrenheit.
- The evaporation point of THC is 380° Fahrenheit.
- There are approximately 1,050 drops in a 1-ounce tincture bottle.

# "Introduction to the Endocannabinoid System," by Dustin Sulak, DO

As you read this review of the scientific literature regarding the therapeutic effects of cannabis and cannabinoids, one thing will become quickly evident: cannabis has a profound influence on the human body. This one herb and its variety of therapeutic compounds seem to affect every aspect of our bodies and minds. How is this possible?

In my integrative medicine clinic in central Maine, we treat over a thousand patients with a huge diversity of diseases and symptoms. In one day I might see cancer, Crohn's disease, epilepsy, chronic pain, multiple sclerosis, insomnia, Tourette's syndrome and eczema, just to name a few. All of these conditions have different causes, different physiologic states, and vastly different symptoms. The patients are old and young. Some are undergoing conventional therapy. Others are on a decidedly alternative path. Yet despite their differences, almost all of my patients would agree on one point: cannabis helps their condition.

As a physician, I am naturally wary of any medicine that purports to cure-all. Panaceas, snake-oil remedies, and expensive fads often come and go, with big claims but little scientific or clinical evidence to support their efficacy. As I explore the therapeutic potential of cannabis, however, I find no lack of evidence. In fact, I find an explosion of scientific research on the therapeutic potential of cannabis, more evidence than one can find on some of the most widely used therapies of conventional medicine.

At the time of writing, a PubMed search for scientific journal articles published in the last 20 years containing the word "cannabis" revealed 7,704 results. Add the word "cannabinoid, " and the results increase to 15,899 articles. That's an average of more than two scientific publications per day over the last 20 years! These numbers not only illustrate the present scientific interest and financial investment in understanding more about cannabis and its components, but they also emphasize the need for high quality reviews and summaries such as the document you are reading.

How can one herb help so many different conditions? How can it provide both palliative and curative actions? How can it be so safe while offering such powerful effects? The search to answer these questions has led scientists to the discovery of a previously unknown physiologic system, a central component of the health and healing of every human and almost every animal: the endocannabinoid system.

## What Is the Endocannabinoid System?

The endogenous cannabinoid system, named after the plant that led to its discovery, is perhaps the most important physiologic system involved in establishing and maintaining human health. Endocannabinoids and their receptors are found throughout the body: in the brain, organs, connective tissues, glands, and immune cells. In each tissue, the cannabinoid system performs different tasks, but the goal is always the same: homeostasis, the maintenance of a stable internal environment despite fluctuations in the external environment.

Cannabinoids promote homeostasis at every level of biological life, from the subcellular, to the organism, and perhaps to the community and beyond. Here's one example: autophagy, a process in which a cell sequesters part of its contents to be self-digested and recycled, is mediated by the cannabinoid system. While this process keeps normal cells alive, allowing them to maintain a balance between the synthesis, degradation, and subsequent recycling of cellular products, it has a deadly effect on malignant tumor cells, causing them to consume themselves in a programmed cellular suicide. The death of cancer cells, of course, promotes homeostasis and survival at the level of the entire organism.

Endocannabinoids and cannabinoids are also found at the intersection of the body's various systems, allowing communication and coordination between different cell types. At the site of an injury, for example, cannabinoids can be found decreasing the release of activators and sensitizers from the injured tissue, stabilizing the nerve cell to prevent excessive firing, and calming nearby immune cells to prevent release of pro-inflammatory substances. Three different mechanisms of action on three different cell types for a single purpose: minimize the pain and damage caused by the injury.

The endocannabinoid system, with its complex actions in our immune system, nervous system, and all of the body's organs, is literally a bridge between body and mind. By understanding this system we begin to see a mechanism that explains how states of consciousness can promote health or disease.

In addition to regulating our internal and cellular homeostasis, cannabinoids influence a person's relationship with the external environment. Socially, the administration of cannabinoids clearly alters human behavior, often promoting sharing, humor, and creativity. By mediating neurogenesis, neuronal plasticity, and learning, cannabinoids may directly influence a person's open-mindedness and ability to move beyond limiting patterns of thought and behavior from past situations. Reformatting these old patterns is an essential part of health in our quickly changing environment.

## What Are Cannabinoid Receptors?

Sea squirts, tiny nematodes, and all vertebrate species share the endocannabinoid system as an essential part of life and adaptation to environmental changes. By comparing the genetics of cannabinoid receptors in different species, scientists estimate that the endocannabinoid system evolved in primitive animals over 600 million years ago.

While it may seem we know a lot about cannabinoids, the estimated twenty thousand scientific articles have just begun to shed light on the subject. Large gaps likely exist in our current understanding, and the complexity of interactions between various cannabinoids, cell types, systems and individual organisms challenges scientists to think about physiology and health in new ways. The following brief overview summarizes what we do know.

Cannabinoid receptors are present throughout the body, embedded in cell membranes, and are believed to be more numerous than any other receptor system. When cannabinoid receptors are stimulated, a variety of physiologic processes ensue. Researchers have identified two cannabinoid receptors: CB1, predominantly present in the nervous system, connective tissues, gonads, glands, and organs; and CB2, predominantly found in the immune system and its associated structures. Many tissues contain both CB1 and CB2 receptors, each linked to a different action. Researchers speculate there may be a third cannabinoid receptor waiting to be discovered.

Endocannabinoids are the substances our bodies naturally make to stimulate these receptors. The two most well understood of these molecules are called anandamide and 2-arachidonoylglycerol (2-AG). They are synthesized on-demand from cell membrane arachidonic acid derivatives, have a local effect and short half-life before being degraded by the enzymes fatty acid amide hydrolase (FAAH) and monoacylglycerol lipase (MAGL).

Phytocannabinoids are plant substances that stimulate cannabinoid receptors. Delta-9-tetrahydrocannabinol, or THC, is the most psychoactive and certainly the most famous of these substances, but other cannabinoids such as Cannabidiol (CBD) and Cannabinol (CBN) are gaining the interest of researchers due to a variety of healing properties. Most Phytocannabinoids have been isolated from cannabis sativa, but other medical herbs, such as Echinacea purpura, have been found to contain non-psychoactive cannabinoids as well.

Interestingly, the marijuana plant also uses THC and other cannabinoids to promote its own health and prevent disease. Cannabinoids have antioxidant properties that protect the leaves and flowering structures from ultraviolet radiation—cannabinoids neutralize the harmful free radicals generated by UV rays, protecting the cells. In humans, free radicals cause aging, cancer, and impaired healing. Antioxidants found in plants have long been promoted as natural supplements to prevent free radical harm.

Laboratories can also produce cannabinoids. Synthetic THC, marketed as dronabinol (Marinol), and nabilone (Cesamet), a THC analog, are both FDA approved drugs for the treatment of severe nausea and wasting syndrome. Some clinicians have found them helpful in the off-label treatment of chronic pain, migraine, and other serious conditions. Many other synthetic cannabinoids are used in animal research, and some have potency up to 600 times that of THC.

## Cannabis, the Endocannabinoid System, and Good Health

As we continue to sort through the emerging science of cannabis and cannabinoids, one thing remains clear: a functional cannabinoid system is essential for health. From embryonic implantation on the wall of our mother's uterus, to nursing and growth, to responding to injuries, endocannabinoids help us survive in a quickly changing and increasingly hostile environment. As I realized this, I began to wonder: can an individual enhance his/her cannabinoid system by taking supplemental cannabis? Beyond treating symptoms, beyond even curing disease, can cannabis help us prevent disease and promote health by stimulating an ancient system that is hard-wired into all of us?

I now believe the answer is yes. Research has shown that small doses of cannabinoids from marijuana can signal the body to make more endocannabinoids and build more cannabinoid receptors. This is why many first-time marijuana users don't feel an effect, but by their second or third time using the herb they have built more cannabinoid receptors and are ready to respond. More receptors increase a person's sensitivity to cannabinoids; smaller doses have larger effects, and the individual has an enhanced baseline of endocannabinoid activity. I believe that small, regular doses of marijuana might act as a tonic to our most central physiologic healing system.

Many physicians cringe at the thought of recommending a botanical substance, and are outright mortified by the idea of smoking a medicine. Our medical system is more comfortable with single, isolated substances that can be swallowed or injected. Unfortunately, this model significantly limits the therapeutic potential of cannabinoids.

Unlike synthetic derivatives, herbal marijuana may contain over one hundred different cannabinoids, including THC, which all work synergistically to produce better medical effects and less side effects than THC alone. While marijuana is safe and works well when smoked, many patients prefer to use a vaporizer or cannabis tincture. Scientific inquiry and patient testimonials both indicate that herbal marijuana has superior medical qualities to synthetic cannabinoids.

In 1902 Thomas Edison said, "There were never so many able, active minds at work on the problems of disease as now, and all their discoveries are tending toward the simple truth that you can't improve on nature." Cannabinoid research has proven this statement is still valid.

So, is it possible that medical marijuana could be the most useful remedy to treat the widest variety of human diseases and conditions, a component of preventative healthcare, and an adaptive support in our increasingly toxic, carcinogenic environment? Yes. This was well known to the indigenous medical systems of ancient India, China, and Tibet, and as you will find in this report, is becoming increasingly well known by Western science. Of course, we need more human-based research studying the effectiveness of marijuana, but the evidence base is already large and growing constantly, despite the DEA's best efforts to discourage cannabis-related research.

Does your doctor understand the benefit of medical cannabis? Can he or she advise you in the proper indications, dosage, and route of administration? Likely not. Despite the two largest physician associations (American Medical Association and American College of Physicians) calling for more research, the Obama administration promising not to arrest patients protected under state medical cannabis laws, a 5,000 year history of safe therapeutic use, and a huge amount of published research, most doctors know little or nothing about medical cannabis.

This is changing, in part because the public is demanding it. People want safe, natural and inexpensive treatments that stimulate our bodies' ability to self-heal and help our population improve its quality of life. Medical cannabis is one such solution. This summary is an excellent tool for spreading the knowledge and helping to educate patients and healthcare providers on the scientific evidence behind the medical use of cannabis and cannabinoids.

This material originally appeared in the publication, Emerging Clinical Applications for Cannabis & Cannabinoids, published by the National Organization for the Reform of Marijuana Laws (norml.org). A version of this publication is available online at: http://norml.org/library/recent-research-on-medical-marijuana.

Made in the USA
San Bernardino, CA
12 January 2020